RUNNING THE TWIN CITIES

Where to do it:
Routes to run, winter and summer
Where to go when you're finished
Where to find competition

by Gretchen Kreuter

Illustrated by Kent Kreuter

Copyright 1980 Nodin Press Inc.,
a division of Micawber Inc.
519 North Third St., Minneapolis, minn. 55401
Printed in U.S.A. at the
North Central Publishing Company, St. Paul
All rights reserved.
First Printing
ISBN 0-931714-08-7

TABLE OF CONTENTS

ACKNOWLEDGMENTS 5
INTRODUCTION 7
KEY 8

MINNEAPOLIS RUNS

    Downtown-Loring-Isles 11
    Women's History 13
    The Lakes 15
    Lake Harriet 17
    Prairie South 19
    Prairie North 23
    Lake Calhoun 25
    Lake of the Isles 29
    Cedar Lake 31
    Wright to Wright 33
    Victory-Wirth 36
    Wirth-Cedar-Calhoun 39
    Columbia Park 40
    Waite Park Vita Course 41
    Sanford-Comstock 43
    Mississippi River Road 46
    Minnehaha Parkway 49
    Nokomis Fitness 51

ST. PAUL RUNS

    Downtown: Y-Lilydale 55
    Women's History Short Course 57
    Cass Gilbert Run 60
    Fitzgerald's Sleigh Ride 63
    Cherokee Heights 65
    Edgcumbe-Highland 67
    St. Anthony Park-University Grove 69

>   Coliseum 71
>   Como 73
>   Wheelock Parkway 76
>   Lake Phalen 79
>   Johnson Parkway 81
>   Mounds Park 82
> *RESTAURANTS* 85
> *RACES* 89
> *RUNNING CLUBS* 92
> *BIBLIOGRAPHY* 95

ACKNOWLEDGEMENTS

Many people have contributed to this book by expressing interest, suggesting places to run, and contributing their general encouragement. My greatest debt, however, is to Winifred D. Wandersee Bolin, now of Syracuse University. The original idea for the book developed while we were training for our first marathon. Although professional commitments made it necessary for her to leave the Twin Cities area, she has contributed her ideas and enthusiasm by long-distance since her departure. I'd never have finished the marathon, or the book, without her.

Betsy Kreuter took notes, measured distances on her bicycle, ate more veggie meals than she wanted, and suggested the title for the book. David Kreuter and Cheryl Dickson offered advice from the perspective of non-runners. Two of my colleagues at St. Olaf College deserve thanks: Prof. David Wee, who first whetted my interest in distance running, and Prof. James Farrell, who helped with the architectural runs and read portions of the manuscript. The research done by Carol Lacey and Karen Mason on Twin Cities' women's history furnished much of the data for the women's history runs. Mae Horns, Judy Lutter, and Addie Mattson of the Northern Lights Track Club suggested vegetarian restaurants and some running routes. Not all those routes are here. I regretfully decided that suburban locations would have to wait for another book. I'm also indebted to anonymous runners whom I would ask, while we were huffing and puffing through a race, where they liked to do their training.

INTRODUCTION

Every runner probably has a favorite place to run: a two-mile loop in the neighborhood, a hill in the park to improve the quadriceps, or a six or seven-mile course around a lake or two.

There are, however, good reasons to expand one's running horizons, even in the old home towns. New vistas can take one's mind off a stiffening knee or an aching arch. Marathoners-in-training who need a two or three-hour run once a week will find variety exhilarating. Parents who long for a good run when the children want to go picnicking or swimming or skating or skiing will appreciate areas where the interests of both can be combined. And runners, like normal people, will find that the more they know about their city, the more interesting it becomes.

Visitors to the Twin Cities will discover that they can combine sight-seeing with a good run. They'll be able to impress the folks back home with both their bodily fitness and the arcane bits of knowledge they have acquired about Minneapolis and St. Paul.

Then there is the climate. Some places are simply better to run in at different seasons of the year. Lake Calhoun, for example, is a glorious and popular summer running spot. In winter, as the wind sweeps unbroken across it, even Nanook of the North would head for the igloo.

This guidebook attempts to meet all these different needs. Each run includes, in addition to the basic route, information on surface, traffic, aesthetics, degree of difficulty, and where there are toilet facilities and water available. Information is included on how to reach the running area by car, public transportation or, of course, on foot.

Some special interest runs are also included — for example, those that include sites of architectural or historical significance — and on some of the more popular and familiar runs, information other than the conventional is supplied. All good Minneapolitans know, for example, that the Peavey Fountain near Lake of the Isles was a horse watering trough. Only the old timers can tell you that it was rededicated to honor the horses that fell in World War I.

And because running has become part of a whole life-style, this guidebook is a guide to some of the adjuncts of that life-style: vegetarian restaurants, running clubs, and racing schedules.

One of the great attractions of running as a sport is that it lends itself to a variety of goals. This guidebook is designed to do the same.

KEY

Each run includes certain basic information of use to the runner. On some, fairly precise mileage is given: on others, only general estimates can be made. Most of the information on maps and narrative is self-evident. That which isn't is explained below:

> * — Beginning point
> **W.** — Water available
> **T.** — Toilet facilities available

AESTHETICS: This refers chiefly to the visual interest and appeal of a particular run and is scored on a scale from 1–10, ten being the most desirable, 1 being the least. Aesthetic judgments are notoriously personal, but you will probably roughly agree with the evaluations given: hardly anyone would think Wacouta Street more attractive than Minnehaha Parkway, for example.

DIFFICULTY: The difficulty of a run is also scored on a scale from 1–10, one being the easiest, and ten being the most difficult. Degree of difficulty is NOT related to the length of the run, but rather to the terrain — usually hills, sometimes windiness.

WEATHER: It is always with us, and in the Twin Cities it comes in almost as many varieties as there are. One can run in any weather, but in summer, shade is preferable to sunshine, and in winter, sheltered areas are more pleasant than those open to the elements. Notations on weather reflect those concerns.

MINNEAPOLIS RUNS

Downtown-Loring-Isles

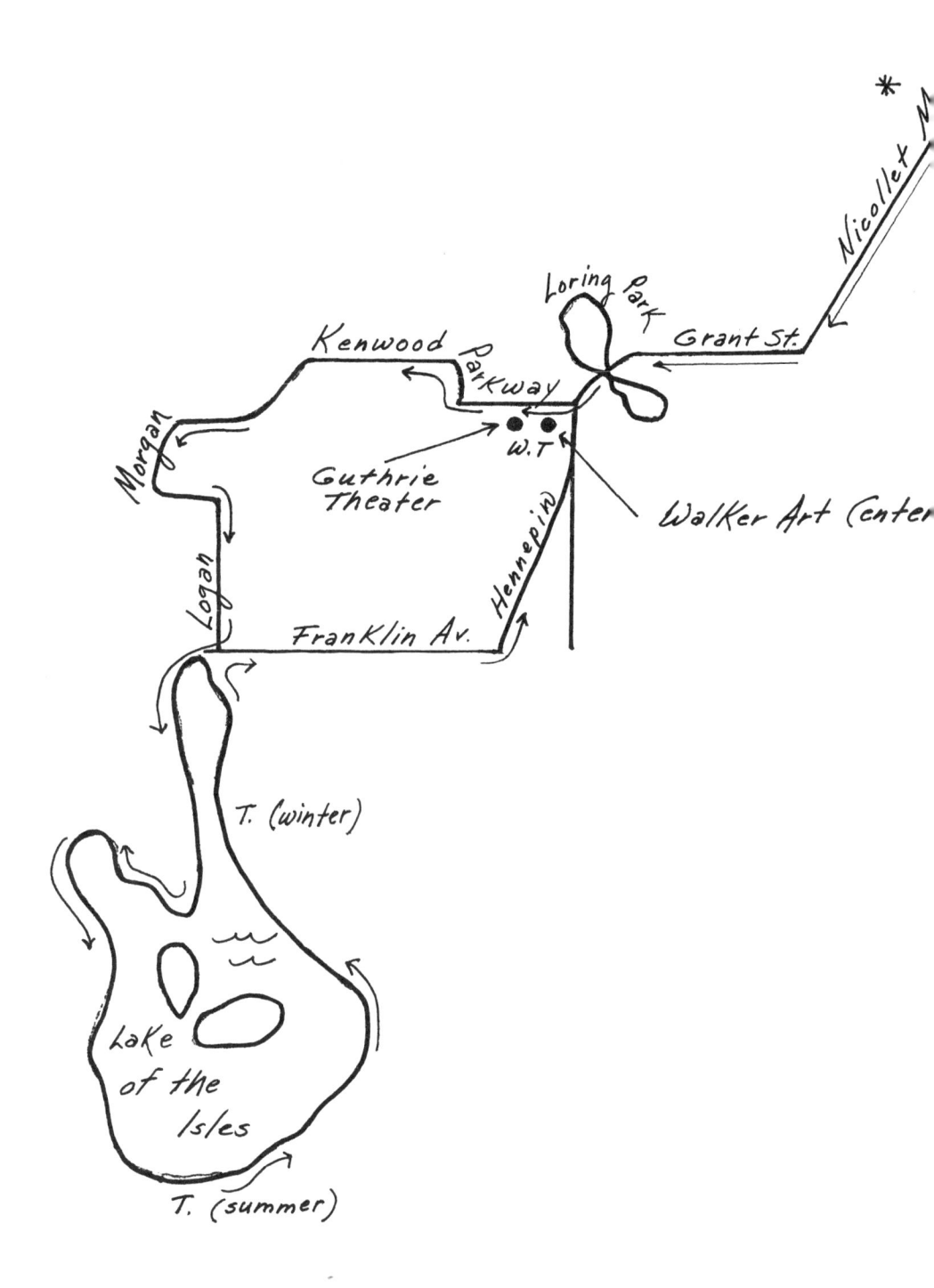

DOWNTOWN-LORING-ISLES

It is not difficult to get from downtown Minneapolis to good running areas. Whether you are working, living, or visiting downtown, head for Nicollet Avenue, or, as it is called along the few blocks where auto traffic is forbidden, the Nicollet Mall. Run south to Grant Street, turn right onto Grant, and you will soon reach Loring Park. This is a pleasant enough park to run, and if you don't have much time you can be content with its lake, bridge, and the delightful Berger Fountain — which looks like a giant dandelion gone to seed.

If you have time other things are close at hand (or, more properly, foot). Run through Loring Park toward the Guthrie Theater, which is on Kenwood Parkway, across the broad busy thoroughfares, Lyndale and Hennepin. Stay on Kenwood, which swings north past the Guthrie, climb a rather substantial hill until you reach Kenwood Park, and little more than 1½ miles from Loring, you will be at Lake of the Isles. You can take a turn around Isles, about 2.8 miles, and return the way you came, or you can turn right onto Franklin Avenue, take Franklin to Hennepin, turn left onto Hennepin, and run north until you reach Loring Park again. The Holiday Inn-Downtown is very near to Loring, as is the Convention Center, and in early 1980 a considerable amount of hotel and residential building was being completed in the Loring Park area. Staying at any of these will place you within easy range of the Minneapolis lake and parkway system. You are not cut off from them by a maze of freeways, as in the case of some cities.

If you're attending meetings downtown, but are not staying at one of the hotels, you can find locker space for your running clothes at the bus depot on First Avenue North, or in the Dayton-Radisson arcade on 8th Street, just off Nicollet Mall. Toilet facilities and water (but not showers) are available at both places. The YMCA, with a 19-lap-per-mile track is at 30 South 9th Street.

DISTANCE: Variable. From Loring-Isles and return, via Franklin, is about 5.5 miles.

BEGINNING POINT: Anywhere along Nicollet Mall

DIFFICULTY: 5

CONDITIONS:

Aesthetics: 3-10

Weather: Mostly shaded, especially the most difficult part, the ascent along Kenwood Parkway.

Traffic: It will slow you down, because of many stop lights as you're leaving downtown. No problem once you're on Kenwood Parkway.

Surface: Asphalt and cement

Women's History: Minneapolis

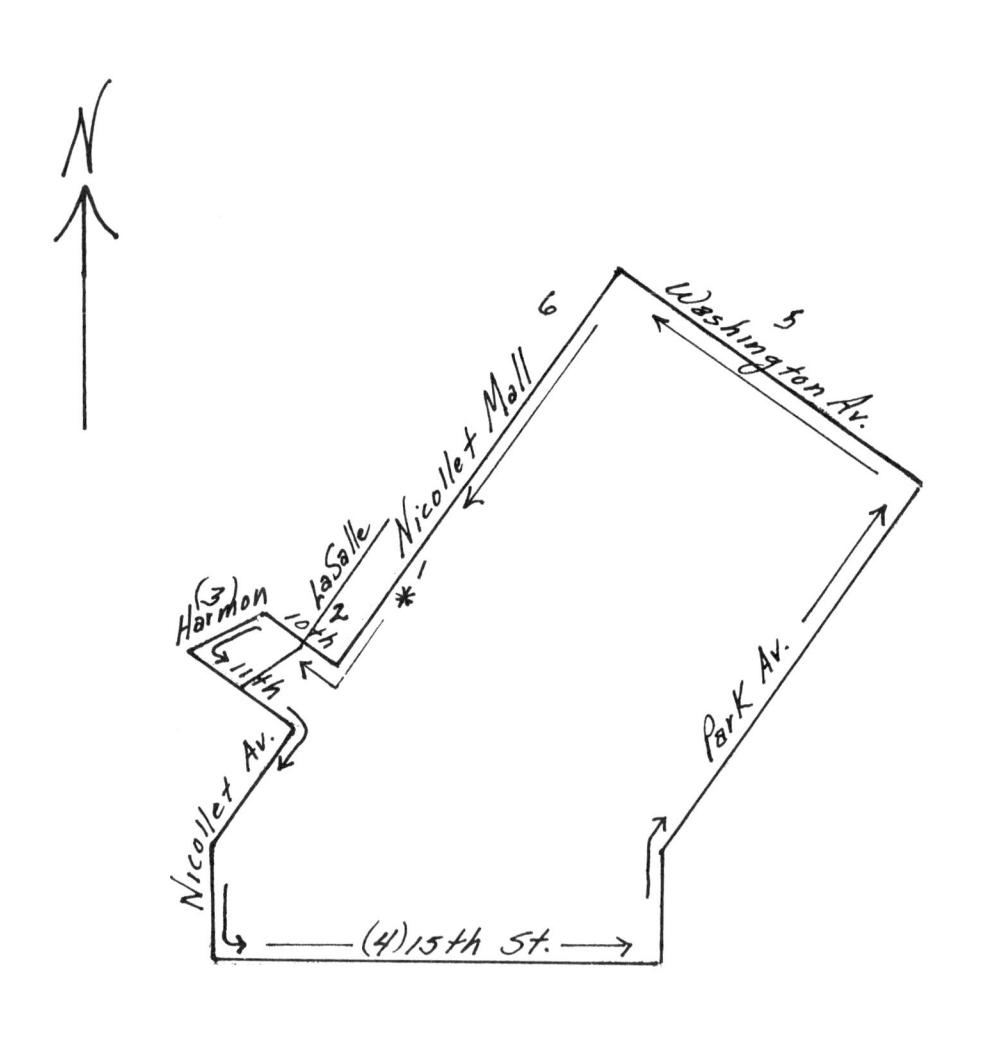

1. Young-Quinlan's
2. Kate Dunwoody Hall
3. First Baptist Church
4. site of Maternity Hospital
5. North Star Woolen Mill
6. Mpls. Public Library

WOMEN'S HISTORY: MINNEAPOLIS

Seedy but safe, is the best way to describe this route which takes you from the heart of the central business district to its fringe areas and back again.

You may begin anywhere along the Nicollet Mall, but an especially good place to start is Young-Quinlan's Department Store at 9th Street. It was co-founded in 1894 by retailer and realtor Elizabeth Quinlan. Successful in what was almost exclusively a man's world, Quinlan worked in a variety of ways to persuade other women to choose non-traditional occupations and thereby reduce the downward pressure of wages in the usual female sectors of the economy.

Turn right onto 10th Street and proceed one block. At 10th and LaSalle you will see the Kate Dunwoody Hall, one of the few remaining residences for working women. The house which was originally on the site was given to the Women's Christian Association in 1905, so that it could shelter young working girls in respectable surroundings and keep them from becoming tarnished doves. A block further on 10th Street, at 10th and Harmon, is the First Baptist Church, site of the 1901 convention of the National American Women's Suffrage Association. All the leaders were there, including Susan B. Anthony and Carrie Chapman Catt. They met in the brick portion of the church, at 11th and Harmon.

Return to Nicollet and continue your run southward to 15th Street. Turn left at 15th and continue to Park Avenue. At what is now a parking lot, but once was 316 15th Street, is the site of Dr. Martha Ripley's Maternity Hospital, the first hospital in Minneapolis that admitted pregnant women without making them first prove that they were married. Dr. Ripley was a long-time foe of the double standard of morality, and a long-time advocate of women's suffrage. It was partly through her influence that the 1901 convention was held in Minneapolis. There is a statue of Dr. Ripley in the rotunda of the state capitol in St. Paul.

Turn left onto Park Avenue. Run northward to the end of Park, at Washington Avenue and the railroad yards. Turn left again, and you will see the old iron train-shed at the Milwaukee Road station — the first sight that greeted the thousands of young women who, beginning in the 1880's, came from farms and villages in outstate Minnesota to work in the factories, mills and offices of Minneapolis. The sight was not uplifting, then or now. Just beyond the railroad yards you will see the tower of the North Star Woolen Mill, where many of those newcomers found jobs.

Washington Avenue in those days was the red-light district where, it was feared, innocent arrivals could be ensnared. To protect them from such a fate, Travelers' Aid matrons, supported by the Women's Christian Association, met trains from early morning until late at night, distributing religious tracts to arriving women and — more to the point — directing them to housing and employment agencies.

When you reach Nicollet, turn left again, and conclude your run by going up the Mall to your starting point. You'll pass the Minneapolis Public Library on your right: the building is comparatively new, but the system is old, and it was shaped chiefly by Gratia Countryman, sometimes called the "Jane Addams of the libraries", who headed the MPL from 1904–1936. The old library building, incidentally, was right next door to the First Baptist Church, up on 10th and Hennepin.

DISTANCE: About 3½ miles

BEGINNING POINT: Nicollet Mall at 9th Street

DIFFICULTY: 1

CONDITIONS:
  Aesthetics: 1
  Weather: No particular problem
  Traffic: This is a downtown run, with lots of traffic lights, so you will probably be delayed more than once.
  Surface: Cement sidewalks

The Lakes

THE LAKES

For most Minneapolitans, running "around the lakes" probably means running around Lake Harriet, Lake Calhoun, and Lake of the Isles, the three that are most closely connected, the three that can be most easily circumnavigated, and the three that best lend themselves to variations of distance. The City of Lakes Marathon is run every October around two of them: four circuits of Calhoun and Harriet equal the official distance, and spectators, by standing near the bandshell at Harriet can see both the grateful finishers and the tortured souls heading for Calhoun and another six-plus miles.

In summer the lakes are a favorite place to run. Runners and bicyclists have separate asphalt paths, although by the summer of 1979 rollerskaters were becoming a real hazard. Most skaters consider themselves foot traffic, but they hurtle along at a pace that would make a runner-skater collision very painful. The paths around the lakes are also flat, and in the summer at least, one can find water and toilet facilities at the north end of Calhoun and Harriet, and toilets at the south end of Lake of the Isles. Winter is another story. There is a toilet near the skating rink on the east shore of Lake of the Isles and a warming house in case you are not generating enough heat of your own.

Unfortunately, the lake paths are indifferently maintained in the winter. Because they are not consistently plowed and swept, they become difficult to run on when alternate thawing and freezing makes them rutted or slushy. As a matter of fact, lakes even if well kept, are not that appealing to run around in the winter. The wind can sweep brutally across them and turn a brisk jog into a struggle for survival. You may tell yourself that such a struggle is "acclimatizing" you — but for what? Few occasions in life, art, or sport call for the tolerance of −50 wind chill.

But this is mere carping. For at least six months out of the year these are beautiful places to run. When your eyes tire of watching the people, the sailboats, and the Canada goslings, you can start looking for the historic sites. This is an area rich in local history. Because each lake has its own distinctive attractions each will be dealt with separately.

A good circuit of all three lakes can be begun at the parking lot near the Lake Harriet bandshell. Circle the lake in either direction. When you get back to the bandshell area, go north along William Berry Drive until you reach Lake Calhoun. Turn right and continue counter-clockwise along its eastern shore. At Lake Street there is a major intersection with a traffic light. Continue north after you cross, and you will soon come to Lake of the Isles. Take this one in a counter-clockwise direction too.

After you cross the bridge over the lagoon on the west side, turn right onto Dean Boulevard, and follow it back to Lake Calhoun. You'll pass the Calhoun Beach Club, the last and sole survivor of several generations of resort hotels that have existed around Lake Calhoun over the past century.

After you cross Lake Street, go up the west side of Calhoun and then back to Harriet on Berry Parkway. There's a picnic ground, a good swimming beach with diving dock, and a concession stand with ice cream, soft drinks, and popcorn, all within a few hundred feet of where you've parked your car. If you're feeling particularly at one with the natural world after your run, you may want to stroll through the Roberts Bird Sanctuary, the entrance to which is just across the street from the bandshell.

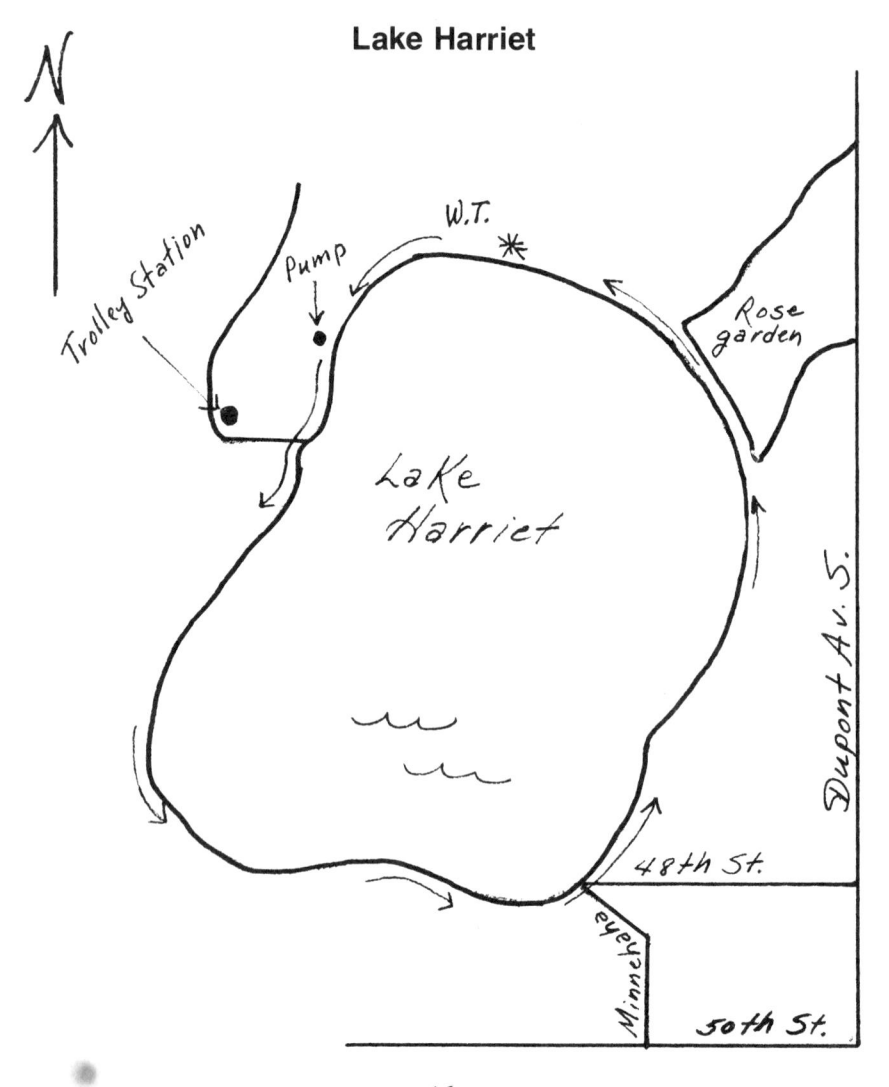

Lake Harriet

LAKE HARRIET

Lake Harriet, slightly less than three miles in circumference, has a variety of activities around its shores. In addition to the usual beach and concession stands, Lake Harriet is adjacent to some other worthy attractions. On summer Sundays, a trolley car of the old Como-Harriet line leaves periodically from its station just up from West Lake Harriet Boulevard. The journey is scarcely over a mile and back, but it's reminiscent of days gone by when this form of public transportation connected downtown Minneapolis with the Calhoun and Harriet neighborhoods.

If you're strolling up to the trolley car station either before or after your run, you may pass the old-fashioned pump where you can treat yourself to a cup or handful of pure cold well water. Several years ago, when the Minneapolis public water system was invaded by harmless but foul-smelling algae, people came from far and near to the Harriet pump to fill jugs and jars of all sizes.

Across the street from the Lake Harriet bandstand is the entrance to the Roberts Bird Sanctuary, a pleasant place to stroll and catch your breath. If you haven't had enough running after a time or two around the lake, you can swing past the rose gardens that are visible from the northeast corner of Harriet. From June until October, they are beautiful. Take time to smell the roses.

DISTANCE: One circuit of Harriet is about 3 miles

BEGINNING POINT: Parking lot at north shore of the lake

DIFFICULTY: 1

CONDITIONS:
  Aesthetics: 8
  Weather: Mostly shaded; windy in winter.
  Traffic: No problem: divided paths for cyclists & pedestrians
  Surface: Asphalt

Prairie School-South

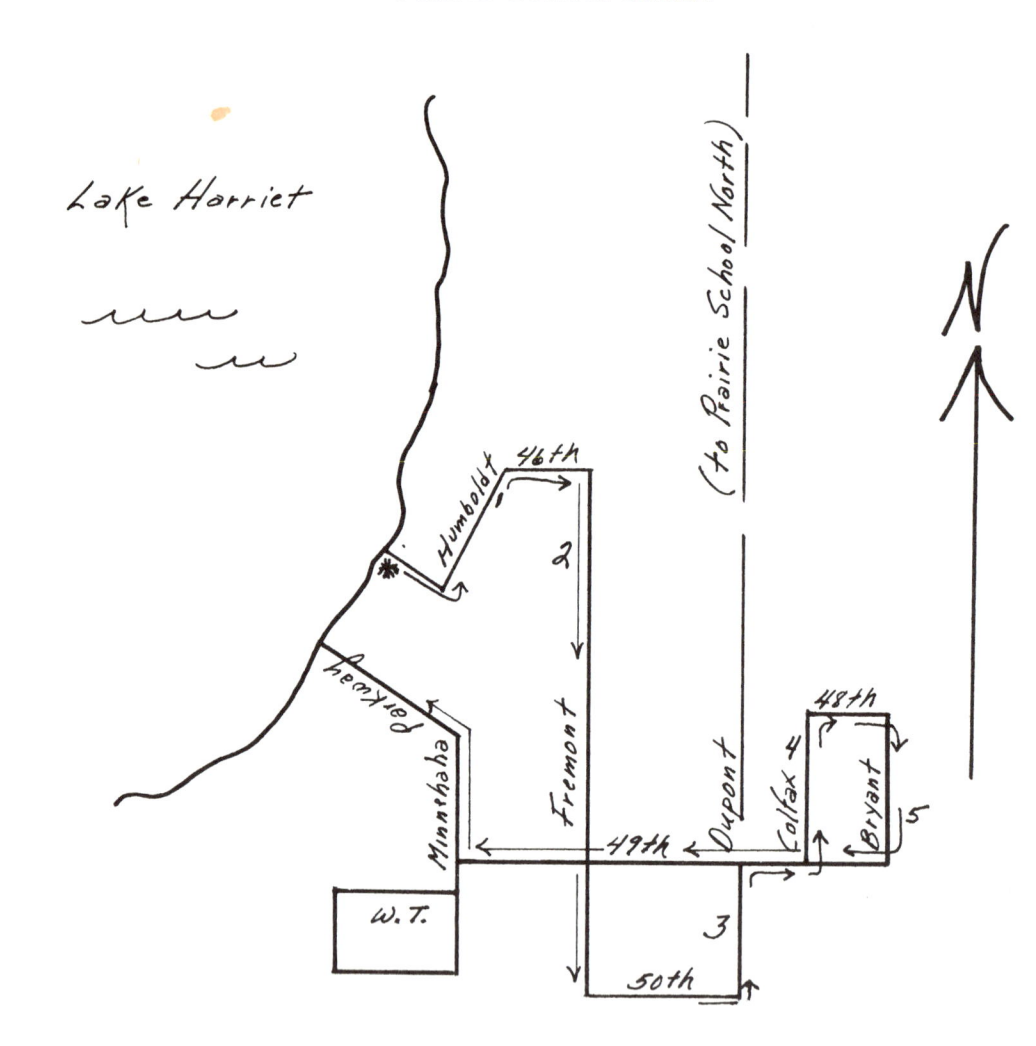

1. 4609 Humboldt
2. 4700 Fremont
3. 4920 Dupont
4. 4829 Colfax
5. 4845 Bryant

Water and toilets are at Lynnhurst Field, a slight detour from the main route.

PRAIRIE SCHOOL RUN: SOUTHERN

When winter comes you may want to look at something other than frozen tundra while you're running. If you do, you can, with little effort, see some of the most distinguished and original domestic architecture in the Twin Cities: the homes designed by architects of the Prairie School and built early in the twentieth century.

Frank Lloyd Wright was the great founding father of the Prairie School. However, with but one exception, the Francis Little home at Lake Minnetonka which has since been razed, he did not design any buildings in the Twin Cities in the pre-World War I period. Most of Wright's commissions here were in the 1930's.

The principles of the Prairie School in Minneapolis were best exemplified in the work of George Elmslie and William G. Purcell. Elmslie was a Scotsman, Purcell a native of Oak Park, Illinois, and the two men worked for a time in Louis Sullivan's architectural firm in Chicago just as Frank Lloyd Wright did. In 1909 Purcell and Elmslie entered into a partnership in Minneapolis, and in the years that followed they received a number of commissions from clients who, happily for the weekend runner, all lived in roughly the same part of south Minneapolis.

What's distinctive about this school of domestic architecture is that it doesn't try to imitate historic architectural styles — whether colonial, English, Mediterranean or Renaissance. Instead, Prairie School homes meet the needs of their owners by imitating natural style. The houses are usually conceived in simple, natural geometric shapes which stress the horizontal lines of the prairie. Low roofs with projecting eaves contribute to this emphasis on the horizontal and help create a psychological "line of repose", designating the home as a place of rest for the family. The shapes take form in materials that emphasize natural colors — often brick or sandy stucco. Large windows, often in strips, open the house to its surroundings, even as the leaded glass assures privacy for the people within. On the inside, wood strips and terra cotta ornament, usually over doorways or on fireplace walls, complete the natural feel.

You probably won't get a chance to see those fireplace walls unless your runner's high has banished your inhibitions and left you capable of peeking shamelessly in the windows or asking at the front door for a glass of water. However, the exteriors of some of these Purcell and Elmslie houses are reward enough for taking the trouble to jog past them. In winter, the lines of the houses are more clearly visible. In summer, the privatizing effect of shrubbery and gardens is obvious.

There are two clusters of Purcell-Elmslie Prairie-style homes in south Minneapolis. One is near Lake Harriet. The other, which actually contains the most distinguished examples, is near Lake of the Isles. If you're out for a long run — about 11 miles round trip — you can see both in a single morning. If that's a little too ambitious, you can see one cluster and then add a loop around the nearby lake to fill out a respectable four or five miles.

Begin on the east side of Lake Harriet, just north of Minnehaha Parkway. There's a parking bay opposite the small beach there. Go up the small flight of steps that takes you up to Humboldt Avenue, and proceed left on Humboldt to 46th Street. At 4609 Humboldt is the Wiethoff House, built in 1917. It features an adaptation of the traditional gable roof form though in this case the gable end is toward the street. Note how the first floor siding ends just beneath the second floor windows, giving the illusion of a compact house.

Turn right at 46th and then right again on Fremont. At 4700 you will pass the Wakefield House (1911), with its massive chimney and simple facade; it's a fine example of the Purcell-Elmslie adaptation of Prairie School ideas.

Continue down Fremont until you reach 50th Street, and then turn left and run up the hill to Dupont. Turn left onto Dupont, and at 4920 you will reach the Hineline House (1910), which has been rather unsympathetically maintained. The stucco is rose-colored; metal awnings at the front windows have a large letter M on them.

Turn right onto 49th Street, then left at Colfax where, at 4829, you will see the parker House (1912-13), done in white stucco and well kept. It has a superb set of strip windows and a protective brick porch which embraces the home.

Turn right onto 48th Street, then left at Bryant, and at 4845 you will see (just barely) perhaps the most interesting home among this cluster of Purcell-Elmslie buildings. It is the Mueller Studio (1910-11), a small, low, board-and-batten building originally located in a grove of pines here. Initially it served as a studio and office for Paul Mueller, a landscape architect whose home was up on Aldrich Avenue. The studio, now a single-family home, is well-concealed from the street, and though the pines are gone they have been replaced by other trees that serve to privatize the site. Of all the Prairie School houses in this area, the Mueller Studio is perhaps most reminiscent of Frank Lloyd Wright. Like Wright's own Taliesen, it is built into the brow of a hill.

The rest of your route is simple. Continue down Bryant to the corner, and turn right onto 49th Street. From here you can either continue down 49th to Minnehaha Parkway and then go back to Lake Harriet for turn around the lake, or you can turn right onto Dupont, and head north to the northern cluster of Prairie School homes around Lake of the Isles.

DISTANCE: 2 miles; 4.5 with loop of Lake Harriet added

BEGINNING POINT: Parking bay at beach, east shore of Lake Harriet

DIFFICULTY: 3: modest hill eastbound

CONDITIONS:
  Aesthetics: 7
  Weather: Shaded and residential; sheltered from wind and sun
  Traffic: No problem
  Surface: Cement and asphalt

Prairie School-North

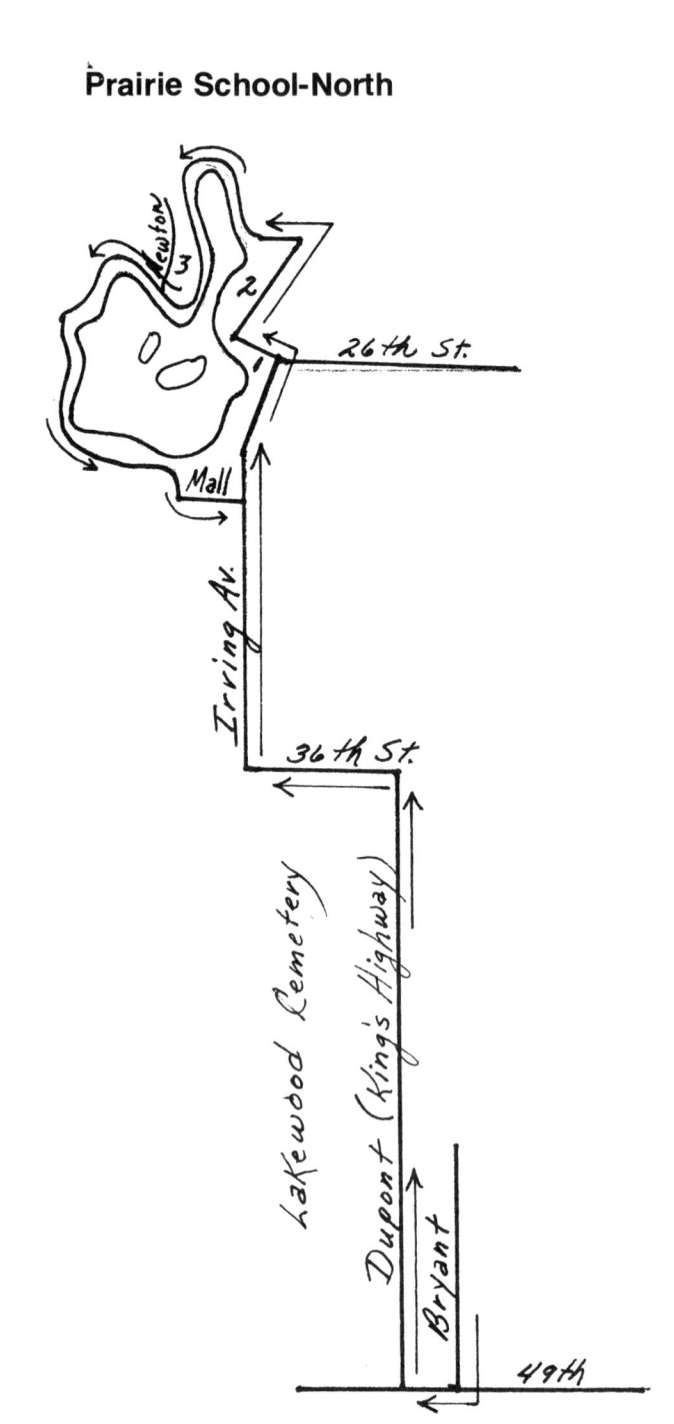

N ↑

1. Powers House: 1635 W. 26th
2. Purcell House: 2328 Lake Place
3. Owre House: 2625 Newton

PRAIRIE SCHOOL: NORTH TO ISLES

If you're going to take in the northern sites of the Prairie School, turn right onto 49th and then right again onto Dupont after you have seen the 5th house on the Prairie School-South run.

Continue down Dupont, along the edge of Lakewood Cemetery, until you reach 36th, where you make a left turn. At this corner, you can see the grave of Hubert Humphrey inside the cemetery. (Incidentally, a number of noteworthy citizens are buried in Lakewood: some of them are Floyd B. Olson, a Farmer-Labor governor in the 1930's; Charles Loring, the father of the Minneapolis park system; and Mary Stevens, the first white child born in Minneapolis.) Run down 36th to Irving. You will discover perhaps with dismay, that the orderly alphabetical procession of streets hits a snag here, and presents you with three "H's" in a row: Hennepin, Holmes, and Humboldt. But Irving appears at last: turn right onto it, and continue along Irving until you reach 26th. Turn left onto 26th and continue to 1635 W. 26th, the Powers House, which will be on your left.

The E. L. Powers home was built in 1910 and is still in excellent condition. In order to accommodate the narrow lot, the house is essentially turned sidewise, with the den, dining room, and kitchen at the front. It has a spectacular fireplace inside, with terra cotta ornament about it. One may wistfully note that the house cost $17,500 to build. When the house was on the market in 1978, the asking price was $250,000.

Just beyond the Powers House is the corner of 26th and Lake Place. Turn right on Lake Place, and proceed to 2328, which will be on your left. This dwelling, the Purcell House built in 1913, is really the finest jewel of Purcell and Elmslie's work in the Twin Cities and one of the greatest Prairie School houses in the United States. It is set far back from the street on a narrow lot. The main floor is a single space of different levels, and from the rear there was once a view of Lake of the Isles, now obscured by subsequent building.

After you've paused respectfully at the Purcell House, continue along Lake Place to 22nd, turn left onto 22nd, and run down to Lake of the Isles. (If the winter gales are too severe, you can, of course, simply retrace your steps from 2328, and skip the circuit of Isles.) Turn right, and follow the lake path around. You may want to take one slight detour at Newton Avenue, before you reach the canoe racks, and have a look at the Owre Residence at 2625 Newton. It is one of the largest houses built by Purcell and Elmslie, and it is sited to take advantage of the lake view.

Instead of following Isles all the way around, turn left at East Isles Boulevard, go under a cement railroad bridge, and then turn left at Mall. Mall leads to Irving; turn right onto Irving, run Irving to 36th, 36th to Dupont, Dupont to 49th, and back to your starting point at Lake Harriet.

DISTANCE: 11 miles

BEGINNING POINT: Parking bay at beach, east shore of Lake Harriet

DIFFICULTY: 5; some hills along Dupont

CONDITIONS:
  Aesthetics: 7
  Weather: Shaded and residential; sheltered from wind and sun, except around part of Lake of the Isles.
  Traffic: No problem
  Surface: Cement and asphalt

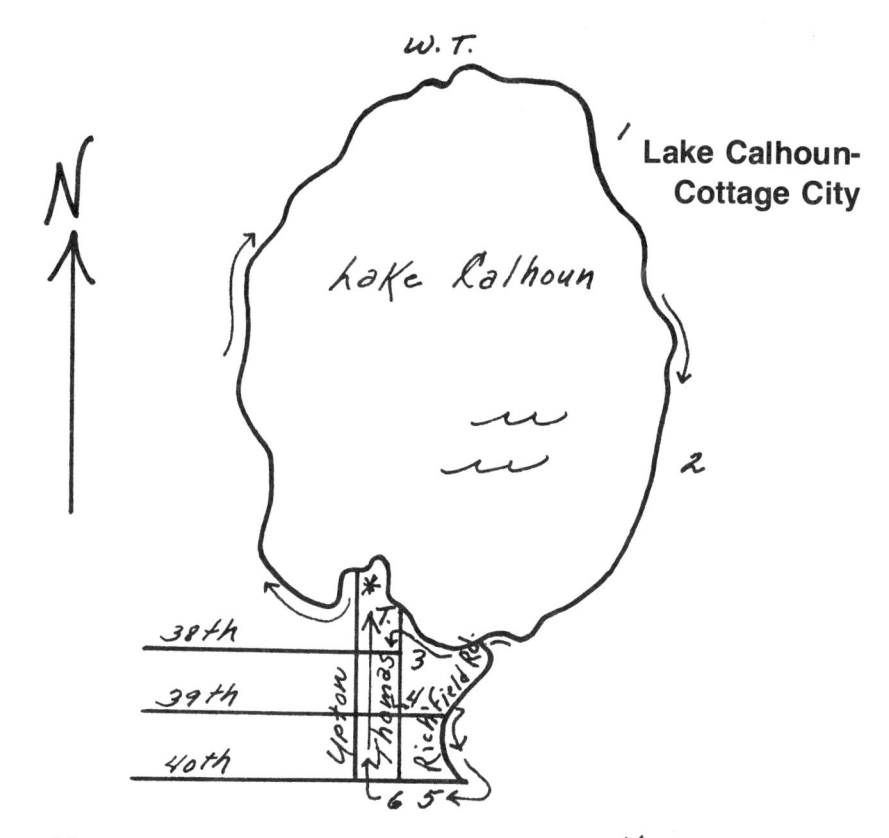

1. Mast and bell, Battleship Minneapolis
2. Marker commemorating site of Ponds' cabin.
3. 3807 Thomas
4. 3823 Thomas
5. 2617 40th
6. 2621 40th

LAKE CALHOUN

Lake Calhoun is 3.1 miles in circumference, which means that two circuits of the lake equal exactly 10 kilometers, a popular running distance. At least one 10K is held at Calhoun each summer, and if you're thinking of trying to establish a new personal record at this distance, you are most likely to do it here. The course is virtually flat.

When you're not racing around Calhoun, you may want to take note of some of its history. The first settlers at the lake were Dakota Indians, the band of Chief Cloudman which located there in the late 1820's. They were followed not many years later by two lay missionaries, the

Pond brothers, Samuel and Gideon. Their cabin was the first dwelling in what is now Minneapolis and its site, high on the hill along the east shore of Calhoun, was chosen by Cloudman himself. From there, he said, they could see the loons on the lake. At 35th and Lake Calhoun Boulevard there is a bronze tablet commemorating the place where the Ponds' cabin once stood.

At Lake Street and Calhoun Boulevard, where there is a concession stand open in summer and an extensive sailboat anchorage, there is also a ship's mast, on which is hung the bell from the 1893 battleship USS Minneapolis.

If you want to add about a mile to your run, you can detour through an unusual subdivision — Cottage City. Many of the houses here are substantially smaller than those nearby, for its lots were originally 25-feet wide. Some of the homes were built in the late 19th century as lake cottages.

If you began your run at the beach parking lot at Upton Avenue, at the south end of the lake, and ran clockwise around Calhoun, you can add the Cottage City mile by turning left off Calhoun Parkway onto Thomas Avenue and continuing down Thomas to 39th. As you pass 38th, you'll see the first of the small houses of this old subdivision, at 3807 Thomas. From 3813 southward you'll pass five cottages, most altered from their original size and facade. The house at 3823, however, retains its original features.

Turn left at 39th and proceed to Richfield Road; then turn right and run down to 40th, turn right again, and proceed along 40th to Upton. Along 40th you'll see, on your left, some of the smallest houses in Cottage City. The home at 2521 was built in 1902, and those at 2617 were built as two separate cottages in 1902 and joined together in 1957. Turn right onto Upton and continue north until you reach the lake and your beginning point.

DISTANCE: 3.1; about 4.0 with Cottage City

BEGINNING POINT: Beach parking lot at Upton and Calhoun Boulevard

DIFFICULTY: 1

CONDITIONS:

   Aesthetics: 5

   Weather: Strong north winds make Calhoun unpleasant on many winter days.

   Traffic: No special problems. There are separate paths for bikers and pedestrians, except in Cottage City, where there are sidewalks.

   Surface: Asphalt and cement

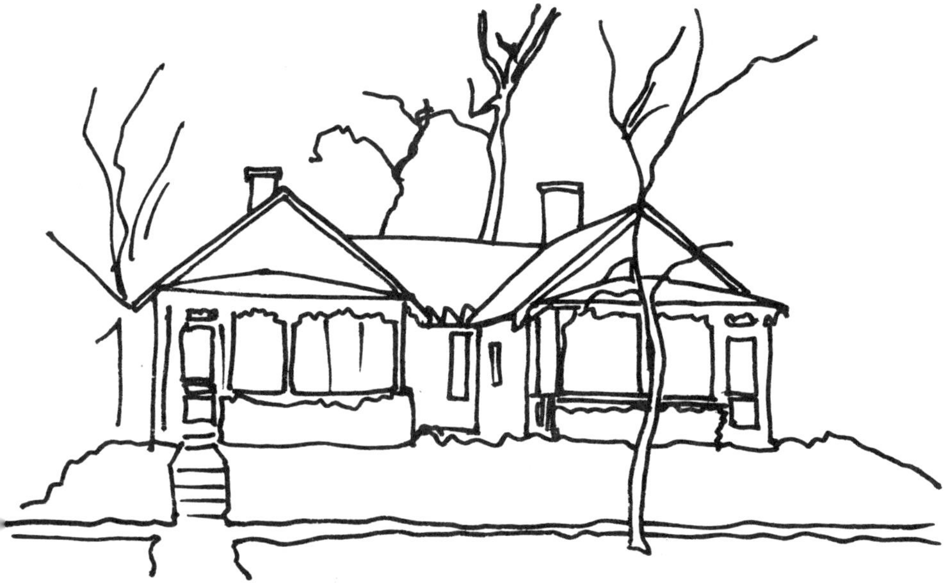

Lake of the Isles

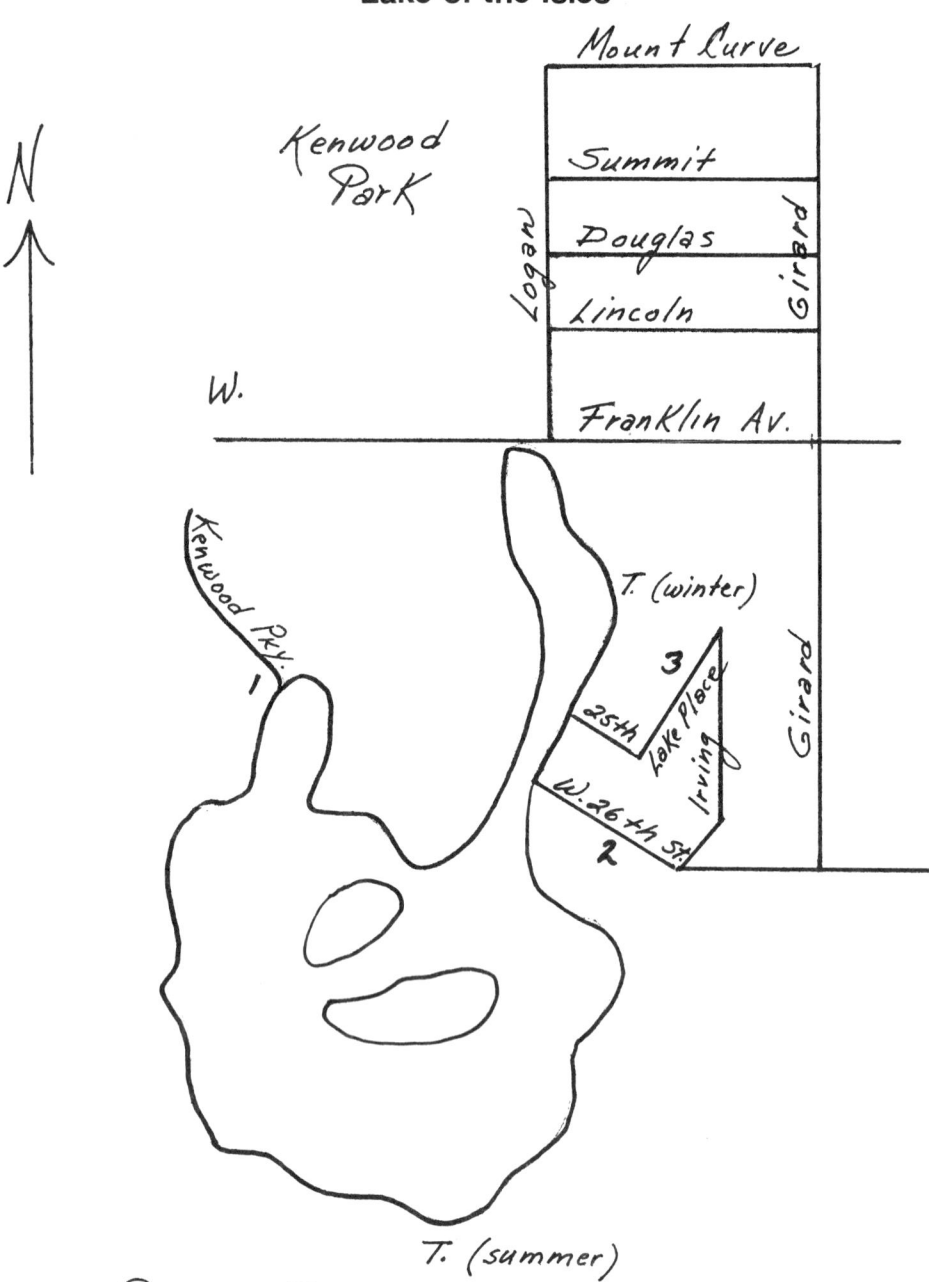

Mount Curve

Kenwood Park

Summit

Logan

Douglas

Girard

Lincoln

W.

Franklin Av.

Kenwood Pky.

1

T. (winter)

3

25th

Lake Place

Irving

Girard

W. 26th St.

2

T. (summer)

1. Peavey Fountain
2. Powers House: 1635 W. 26th
3. Purcell House: 2328 Lake Place

LAKE OF THE ISLES

Lake of the Isles is one of the most popular running sites in the Twin Cities area, and it is not difficult to see why. The scenery is beautiful, whether you look to the lake and its isles or to the spacious and stately homes that border it.

The two islands themselves were once platted for city lots, but less acquisitive heads prevailed, and they remain as wildlife refuges. Even canoe landings and midnight trysts on their shores are forbidden, with notable if not perfect success. A flock of Canada geese and a retinue of mallard ducks are generally in residence at Lake of the Isles. In winter, skaters and cross-country skiers add color and zest, and at Christmastime, neighbors gather on the frozen shore for a bonfire and carol-sing.

The houses along the lake are of varied periods and styles, and many are well worth slowing down for. Only one house on the west side of the lake, 2002 West Isles Boulevard, was constructed in the nineteenth century. The rest were built either between 1900 and 1914 or in the 1920's. Old-time residents tell the story that one of these houses — many have forgotten which one — remained empty and deserted for ten years because newlyweds quarrelled on their first morning there, walked out in anger, and though finally reconciled never returned. According to local lore, the remains of that first breakfast stayed on the table for years. It must have been hardtack.

The Peavey Fountain is also on the west side of the lake at the intersection with Kenwood Parkway. Constructed as a watering-trough early in the twentieth century, it was later rededicated to the horses who died in World War I.

On the east side of the lake, there are many notable homes. You may want to take a slight detour and see two of the finest Prairie School homes in the area: the Powers House at 1635 West 26th and the Purcell House at 2328 Lake Place. Most notable at 1635 is the arrangement of windows to allow maximum light in the interior. Turn right onto West 26th, left at Euclid Place, left again at Irving, then sharply left once more onto Lake Place. Take a right at the corner of 25th and return to the lake boulevard.

When you reach the north end of Lake of the Isles, you may want to take a further detour and proceed up Logan Avenue to Summit, Douglas or Mount Curve and criss-cross this neighborhood (see map). The houses range in appearance from quiet dignity to elegant excess, but most are worth a look. Girard is an especially fine street to run down.

The only drawback on this course is the lack of drinking fountains. There's one in Kenwood Park, but it's usually turned off or out of order.

DISTANCE: 2.8 miles around Lake of the Isles; extendable by adding adjacent neighborhoods.

BEGINNING POINT: almost anywhere along the lake

DIFFICULTY: 3

CONDITIONS:

Aesthetics: 10

Weather: The course is mostly shaded, and it is somewhat sheltered from winter winds.

Traffic: No problem

Surface: Asphalt and cement

Cedar Lake

CEDAR LAKE

Cedar is about the only Twin Cities lake where public access has not been preserved around its entire circumference. This makes Cedar something of a novelty to run around. Skipping across railroad tracks and scrambling down an embankment are pleasant activities that lend an air of exploration to your running, but they may also make you grateful that such stratagems are not necessary everywhere. One of the curious features about both Cedar and Lake of the Isles is the nearness of railroad tracks to elegant neighborhoods. The two features — railroads and residential elegance — don't ordinarily go together, but they do here.

The best place, probably, to begin a circuit of Cedar is on the west shore where parking, and water and toilet facilities, are available. Run northward along the asphalt path toward the bridge over the channel to Brownie Lake. Instead of going over the bridge, look for the path that leads down to the right to the railroad tracks. Follow the line of the lakeshore along the gravel path. Eventually you'll come around to the east shore, and the path becomes a street, Upton Avenue. Upton curves into West 22nd Street, and then reappears on your right. Continue on Upton to Burnham Road. Turn left onto Burnham, continue south until you reach Cedar Lake Boulevard, which you can follow around to your beginning point. Don't run this one when there is snow cover, because you may do more bushwhacking and mushing than running.

DISTANCE: About 3 miles. Hard to measure.

BEGINNING POINT: West shore

DIFFICULTY: 6-8

CONDITIONS:
    Aesthetics: 7; more if you like trains.
    Weather: Spring, summer, fall only. Can be buggy and hot at north shore in summer.
    Traffic: No problem
    Surface: Asphalt, cement, dirt, gravel

N ← **Wright to Wright**

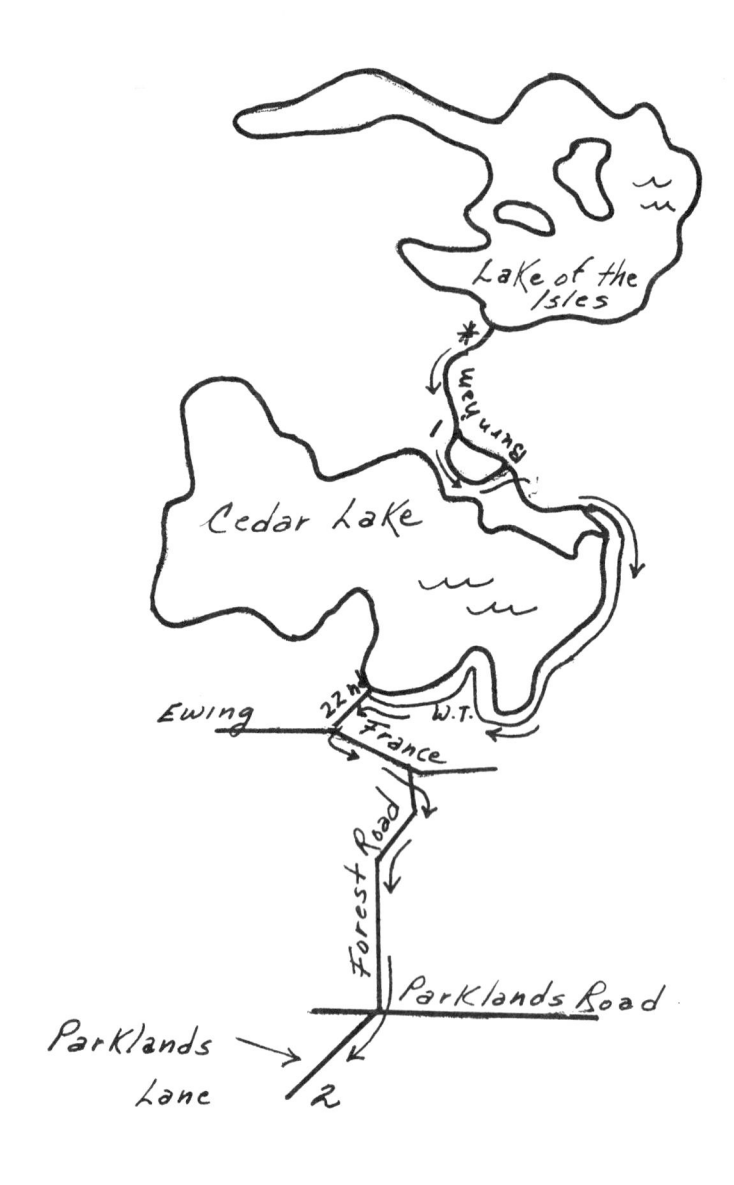

1. Neils Residence: 2801 Burnham Road
2. Olfelt Residence: 2206 Parklands La.

WRIGHT TO WRIGHT RUN

Frank Lloyd Wright, America's greatest architect of the 20th century, did not execute many commissions in the Twin Cities area. One of his houses is in the Prospect Park neighborhood of Minneapolis, on Bedford Street, S.E., overlooking railroad yards and Highway 94. Two Wright homes, both dating from the 1950's, designed very late in the architect's career, may be seen on an attractive four-mile run around Cedar Lake and the Lake Forest subdivision bordering France Avenue.

This is not the place for an analysis of Wright's architecture — a vast literature exists! It is useful to know, however, that one thing he always wanted his homes to provide for his clients was privacy. Therefore you will see only portions of these two homes from the street. Each is sited so there is only one road of access, one view for a passerby. This makes the run no less appealing, because the one road and the one view are well worth seeing. They simply don't provide you with a sense of the totality of the structures.

Begin your run just west of Lake of the Isles. You can park on Sheridan, where Burnham Boulevard begins. After you've crossed a couple of bridges, look for Burnham Road, a small loop off the boulevard. At 2801 Burnham is the Neils House, built in 1950–51. The roofs of the house extend almost to the ground; the walls are of stone and wood. You will see the carport; you will not see the high-angled window that overlooks Cedar Lake.

Continue south on Burnham, to Washburn, and then west around Cedar Lake until you reach West 22nd Street. Turn left onto 22nd, left again when you come to France Avenue (the most visible sign says Ewing, but don't let this put you off: given the tidy alphabetical progression of Minneapolis streets, you know that if Ewing appears, France cannot be far behind.) Soon you will come to Forest Road, a street that takes you into the Lake Forest subdivision, a hilly section of elegant homes sited among trees, creeks, and dead-end streets. Continue along Forest until you reach Parklands Road. Turn right. At once you will see Parklands Lane, a spur leading to the left. At the end of the lane is 2206, the Olfelt House, a hexagonal brick structure with a low gable roof. It was built in 1958–9.

You may want to explore the neighborhood more fully before you head back. Almost any street here is pleasant to run down (or up — there are some nice hills), although you will have to do a fair amount of retracing of steps, because so many of the streets are culs-de-sac. You'll easily find your way back to France Avenue, and the route you came on.

DISTANCE: About 4 miles

BEGINNING POINT: Sheridan Avenue and Burnham Boulevard, just west of Isles

DIFFICULTY: 4

CONDITIONS:

  Aesthetics: 10

  Weather: Shaded and residential, except for part of Cedar Lake, which can be gusty in winter.

  Traffic: No problem, except along France Avenue, where you must run in the street for a couple of blocks. Likewise on Forest Road, but traffic is virtually non-existent here.

  Surface: Asphalt

Victory-Wirth

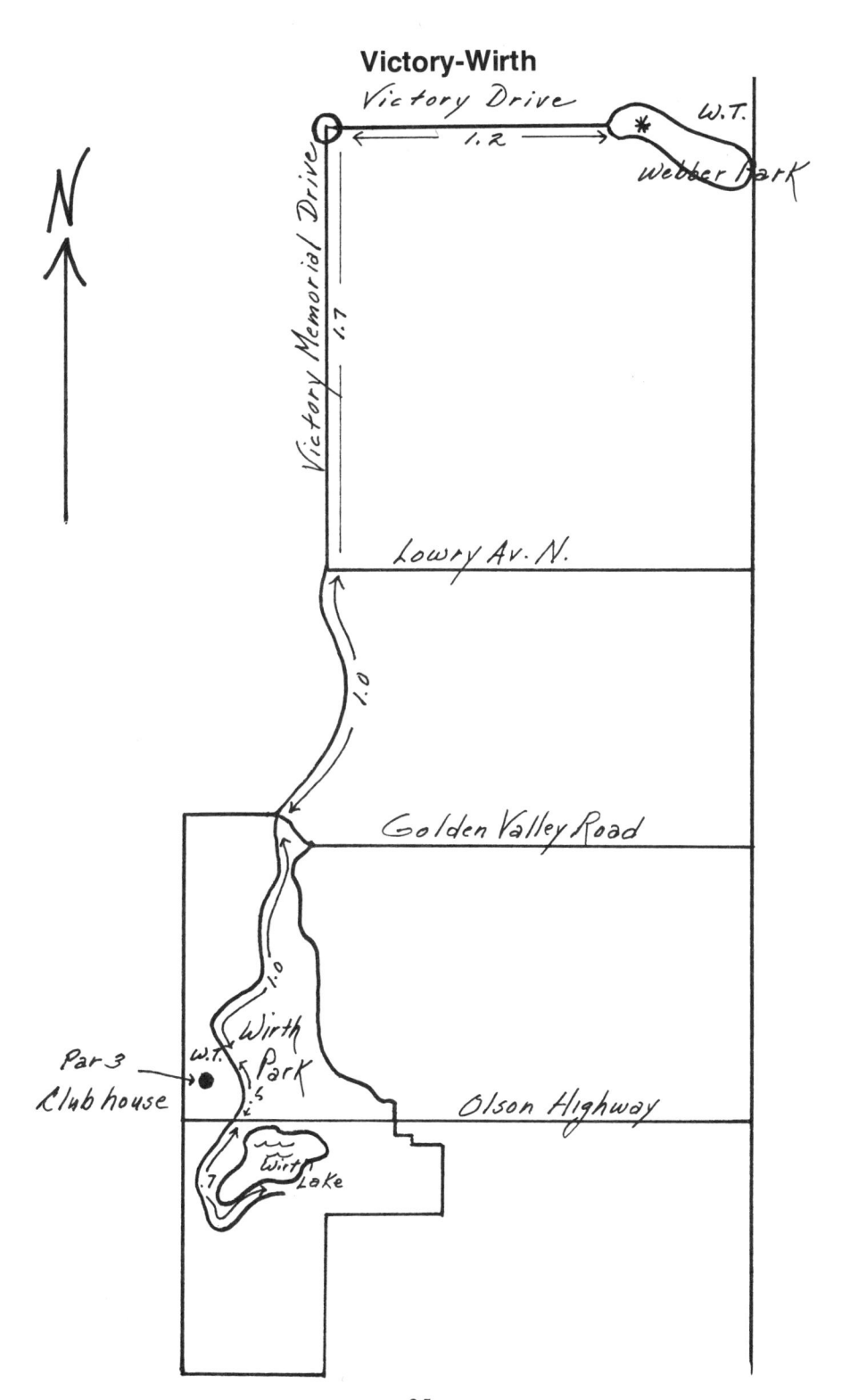

VICTORY MEMORIAL DRIVE-WIRTH

An excellent run through north Minneapolis begins at Webber Park, where there is a parking lot, water, and toilet facilities.

Run east for about 1.2 miles along the asphalt path that follows the boulevard, until you come to the circle with flagpole, dedication, benches and (in summer) flowers. Here the path turns south and becomes hillier and more scenic as you approach Lowry and the northern edge of Wirth Park. There are several nice views along the way, including one of Bassett Creek, which flows through the park.

You may decide that the most welcome view is the Par Three golf club house, about one mile south of Golden Valley Road and nearly five miles from your starting point. (In winter this is the ski touring center in Wirth Park.) The clubhouse has toilets, water, and soft drinks. Slightly more than another mile, and you're at Wirth Lake on Glenwood Avenue.

One of the nice features of this run is that the more difficult portions of it — there are some sizeable hills — occur about halfway along: when you are well warmed up on your way out, and before you are feeling really fatigued on your way back. The first and last miles are flat.

DISTANCE: 12.2 round trip, extendable by adding Wirth-Calhoun or other lake-parkway combinations. For shorter variations, see map.

BEGINNING POINT: Webber Park, 45th Av. N. and Victory Memorial Drive

DIFFICULTY: 5

CONDITIONS:
  Aesthetics: 7
  Weather: No special problems
  Traffic: No problem: separate paths for bikers and pedestrians
  Surface: Asphalt

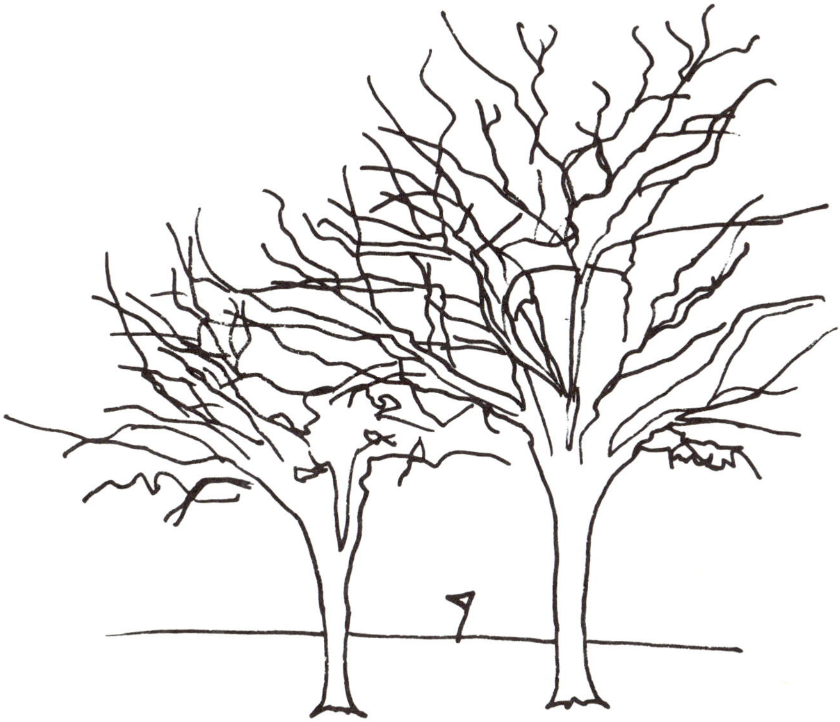

Wirth-Cedar-Calhoun

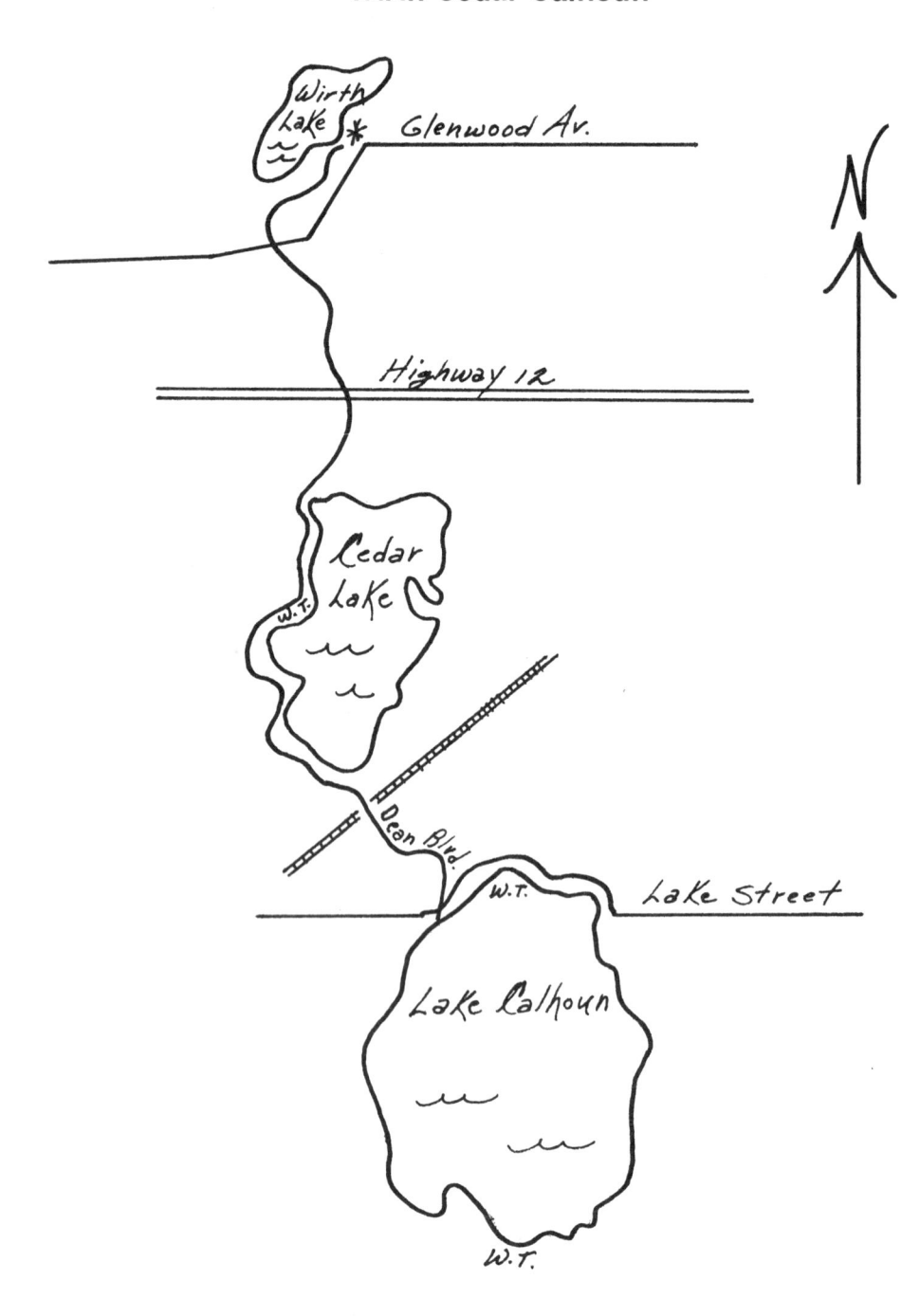

WIRTH-CEDAR-CALHOUN

This run combines some of the woodsier stretches of Wirth Park with the more urban vistas between Cedar and Calhoun.

Begin at the parking lot near the Glenwood Avenue beach at Wirth Lake. There's a picnic ground across the street. Only about .2 of a mile into the run, you'll see the entrance to Eloise Butler Wild Flower Garden, and you may want to make a brief detour to smell the flowers or take a look at the site of the annual spring Mudball Race, sponsored by the Minnesota Distance Running Association.

Continue running along Wirth Parkway, which becomes Cedar Lake Boulevard as soon as you have crossed Highway 12. Along the west side of Cedar Lake you'll find two drinking fountains and one set of toilets. Cross the railroad tracks you come to after running along the south end of Cedar Lake, and continue on the same street until you reach Dean Boulevard. Turn right onto Dean and follow it a short distance to Lake Calhoun. You'll have to cross Lake Street. Traffic is heavy, but there's a stop light, and on the other side, a bathhouse, toilet facilities, and water. If you're still feeling fresh you can add a circuit of Lake Calhoun (3.1 miles) before you start back to Wirth.

DISTANCE: 5.6 miles; 8.7 with loop of Lake Calhoun

BEGINNING POINT: Parking lot, Wirth Beach, off Glenwood Av. N.

DIFFICULTY: 4. There are a couple of good hills.

CONDITIONS:
   Aesthetics: 7
   Weather: Runnable winter and summer. Toilet and water not available in winter.
   Traffic: No problem; divided bike/pedestrian path through Wirth, around Cedar Lake, and along Dean Boulevard
   Surface: Asphalt and cement

Columbia Park

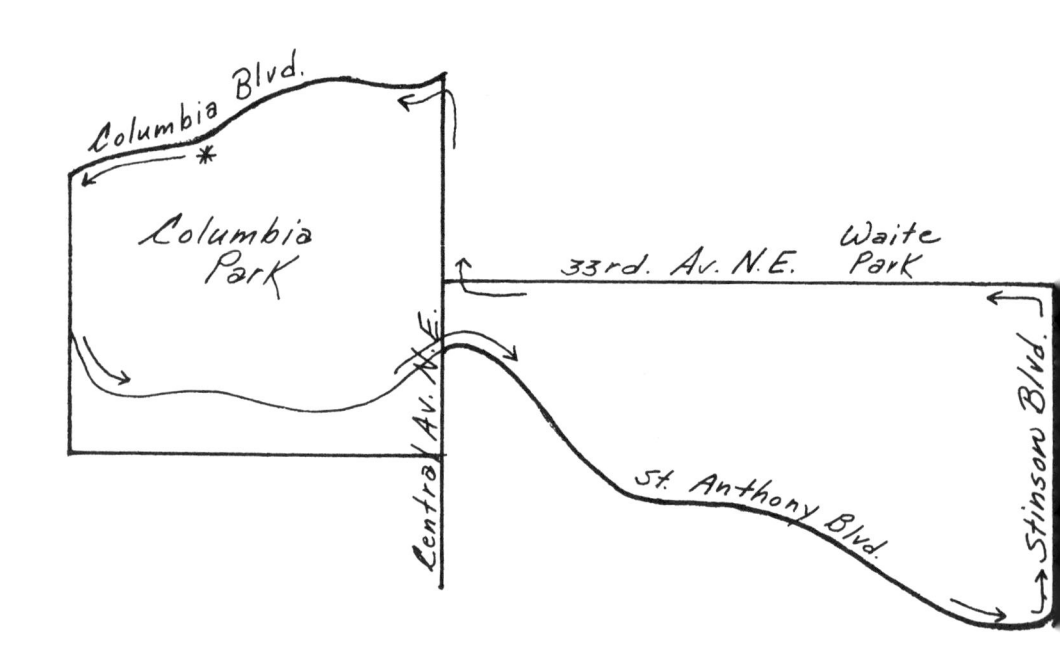

COLUMBIA PARK

Columbia Park in northeast Minneapolis has some of the heftiest hills in town, but fine views of downtown Minneapolis reward you once you have attained their summits. A hilly and varied run of about 5 miles begins at the parking area off Columbia Boulevard. Proceed counter-clockwise along the asphalt path that runs along the edge of the park and golf course. Cross Central Avenue which is the western border of the park, and continue along St. Anthony Boulevard. You'll go up a formidable hill, and then through a pleasant residential neighborhood. When you reach Stinson Boulevard, turn left and run down Stinson to 33rd Avenue N.E., where you should turn left again. Now you're headed back toward Columbia Park. You'll pass Waite Park on your right between Garfield and Ulysses, and you might want to take a detour here and go around the 10-station Vita fitness course at Waite.

In any case, continue on 33rd to Central, then turn right and head north along Central to Columbia Boulevard. Turn left and follow the boulevard back to your beginning point.

DISTANCE: Just under 5 miles; just under 6 with Waite Park addition

BEGINNING POINT: Parking lot off Columbia Boulevard

DIFFICULTY: 8

CONDITIONS:

Aesthetics: 5

Weather: Very gusty and cold on hilltops in the winter; mostly shaded in summer

Traffic: No problem: asphalt pathways in park, sidewalks along residential areas. Traffic regulated by stop lights at busy intersections.

Surface: Asphalt and cement

WAITE PARK

In northeast Minneapolis there is a Vita fitness course in Waite Park. It has only 10 exercise stations, but they are laid out over hillier terrain than at Lake Nokomis, so the course is by no means a pushover. A trip around the Waite Park course might be combined with the Columbia Park run to equal about 6 miles. Excellent play equipment for young children is also in Waite Park.

The park is at 33rd and Ulysses N.E., easily reachable off Stinson Boulevard or Central Avenue N.E. (for map, see Columbia Park run).

Sanford-Comstock

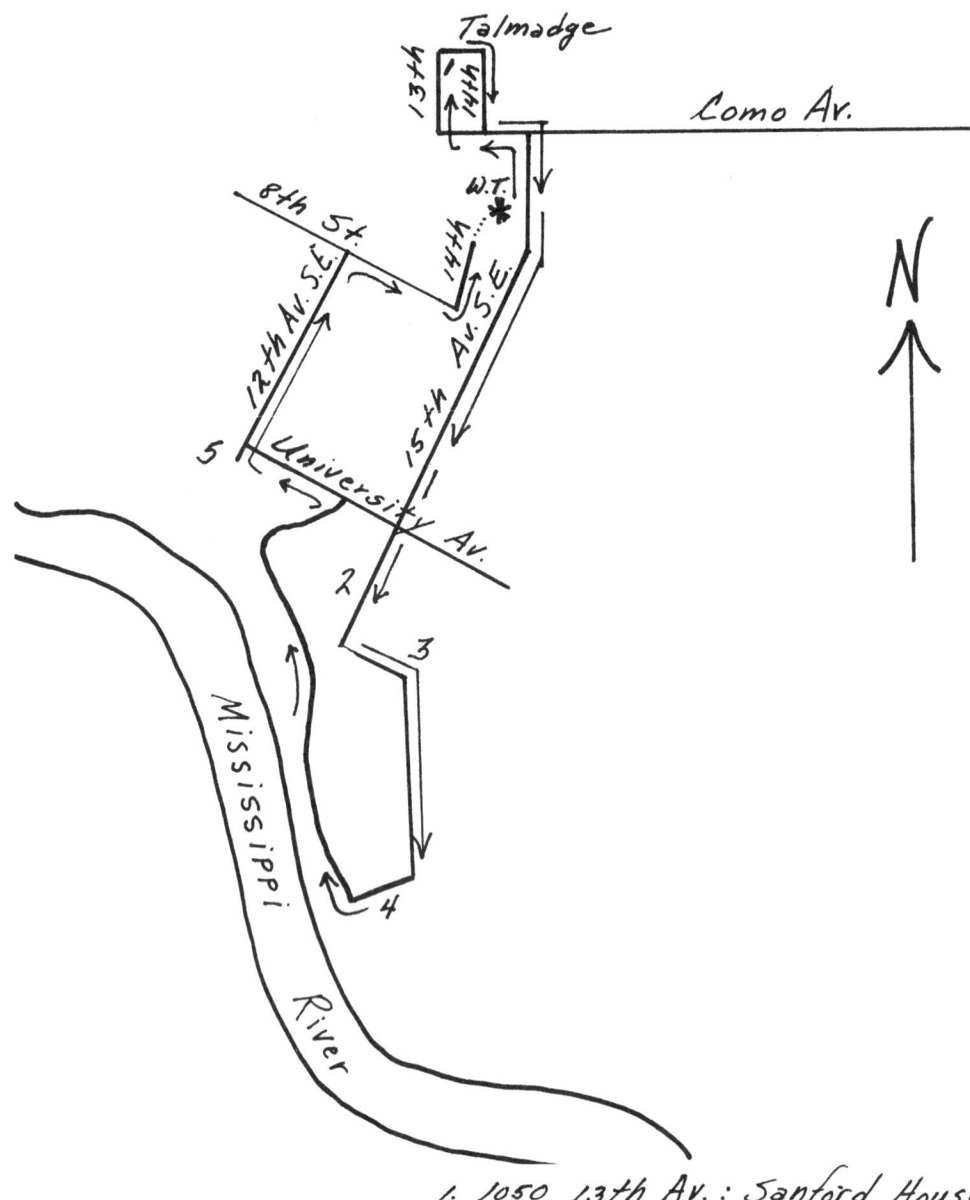

1. 1050 13th Av.: Sanford House
2. Scott Hall
3. Northrup Auditorium
4. Comstock Hall
5. Sanford Hall

SANFORD-COMSTOCK RUN

Two of the most interesting women ever associated with the University of Minnesota were Ada Comstock and Maria Sanford, and you can go on a 3½ mile run through the campus that evokes their memories. Although they were contemporaries and even taught for a time in the same department, they could scarcely have been more different. Ada was to the manor born, daughter of Solomon Comstock, first chairman of the university's Board of Regents. Maria was from a poor but honest New England family, and she was constantly pinching pennies to pay off her father's bad debts or to finance entrepreneurial schemes of her own. Ada married at age 65 — she didn't want marriage to interfere with her career — but she lived to celebrate her silver wedding anniversary with her husband. Maria, unhappily in love with a married man back in Pennsylvania, never wed. Ada went from Minnesota to become Dean of Smith College and then President of Radcliffe, becoming, it was said upon her retirement, "the chief architect of the greatness of this college." Maria, in addition to teaching and tutoring at the university, went on speaking tours to the villages and hamlets of Minnesota, lecturing on classical Greece and Rome before audiences of rural folk. They loved her!

The University of Minnesota has named a dormitory after each one of these formidable women of its early history, but Maria Sanford's own house still stands, and has recently been nominated to the National Register of Historic Places. You can begin your run at Van Cleve Park, at Como and 15th Avenue S.E. Play equipment, ball fields, and water and toilet facilities are here. Go west two blocks on Como to 13th, turn right onto 13th, and proceed to the end of the block. The second house from the corner on your right, with brown trim, an orange door, and unmistakable seediness, is 1050 13th Av. For years Prof. Sanford set out from here each morning to walk to her classes, picking up scraps of paper and other debris as she went. She burned these in her office stove, to save on wood. You will doubtless be moving at a faster clip than she did and therefore will be unable to be quite so thrifty.

Go around the block and return to 15th and Como. Run down 15th into the university campus; 15th becomes Pleasant Ave. here. Several blocks into the campus, you will see Scott Hall on your right. It is named for Verna Scott, manager of the Minneapolis Symphony Orchestra in the 1930's. In those days, the orchestra played in Northrup

Auditorium which you can see by turning left just past Scott Hall and continuing to the mall of the university. Northrup will be on your left, Coffman Union on your right, at the south end of the mall. Run to Coffman, crossing Washington Avenue on the pedestrian bridge. Next to Coffman is Comstock Hall. Run past Comstock, down many steps to the East River Road, following it to the right until it reaches University Avenue. Turn left onto University, and proceed to 12th, where you will see Sanford Hall. It is fitting that the buildings commemorating the two women should be at nearly opposite sides of the campus; as opposite as they were.

From here you can simply return to 15th Avenue and run back to Van Cleve. But you can also run down 12th Avenue to 8th Street, down 8th to 14th Avenue, and up and over a pedestrian bridge that spans the railroad tracks that bisect the area. This will bring forcefully home to you the fact that Maria Sanford lived on the other side of the tracks! But make no mistake, she was a great lady. As the ode composed for her eightieth birthday read:

> Praise her vehement and gusty,
> Praise her kinked and knurled and crusty,
> Leonine and hale and lusty
> Praise her, oaken-ribbed and trusty,
> Shout "Maria" to the skies!

DISTANCE: About 3½ miles

BEGINNING POINT: Van Cleve Park, 15th & Como S.E.

DIFFICULTY: 3

CONDITIONS:

    Aesthetics: 1-5, improving southbound

    Weather: University mall is extremely cold and windy in winter

    Traffic: An occasional stop light. Pedestrian bridges minimize the problems

    Surface: Cement, asphalt

Mississippi River Runs

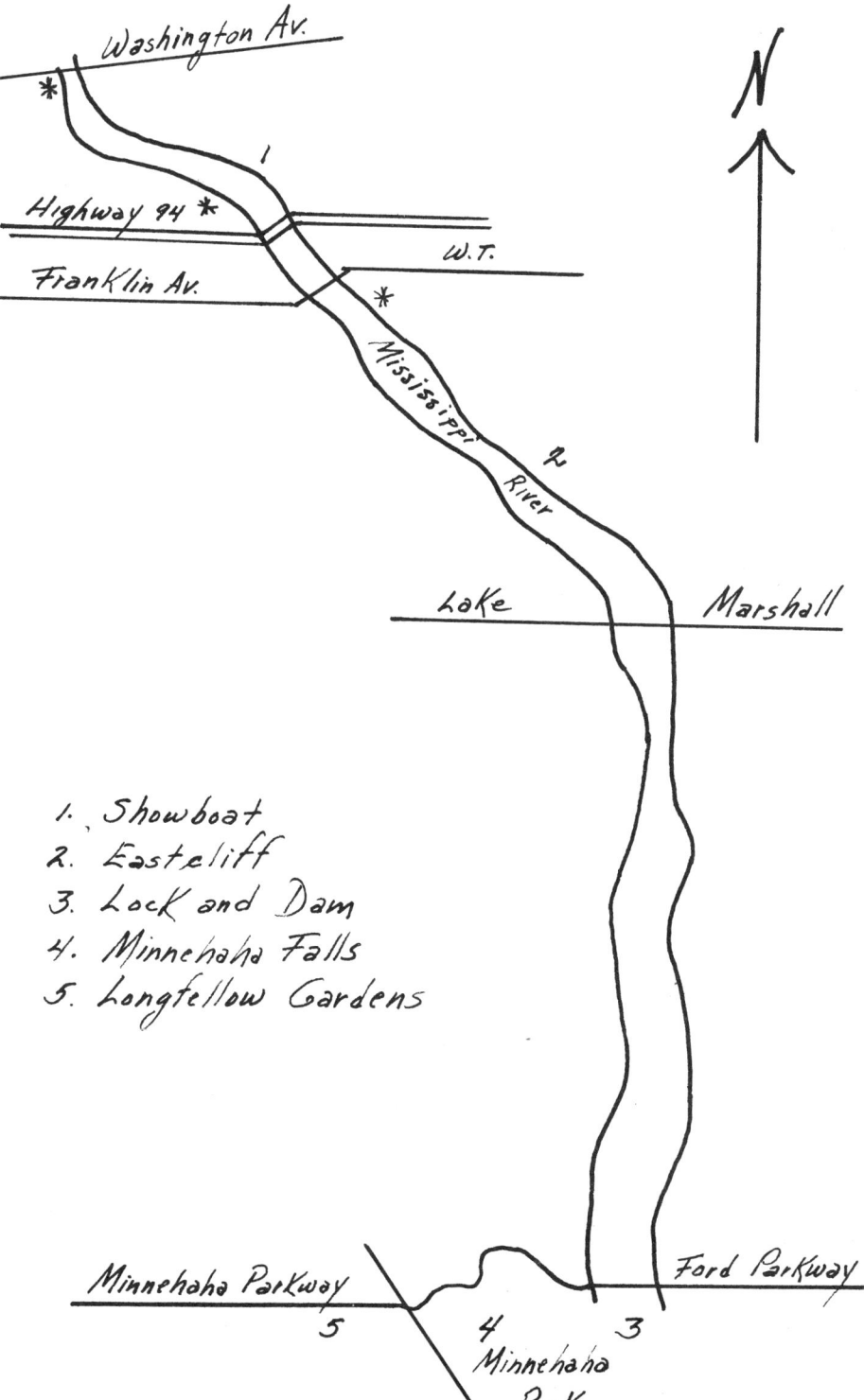

1. Showboat
2. Eastcliff
3. Lock and Dam
4. Minnehaha Falls
5. Longfellow Gardens

MISSISSIPPI RIVER RUNS

This tour will furnish . . . a fair sample of the Great Far West, and the only part of it to which ladies can have access.
George Catlin (1835)

So wrote the American painter George Catlin of the "fashionable tour" of the upper Mississippi. Long before Jimmy Carter gave Mississippi River travel the status of his presidential presence, persons of wealth and leisure, eager for a glimpse of the untamed American interior, traveled upriver and gazed upon forests, bluffs and villages from the decks of stately sternwheelers.

These days, the asphalt River Road, both east bank and west, is far more popular than the watery one. The forests and bluffs are still there. On both banks of the Mississippi, from the Ford Bridge to the University of Minnesota campus, runners may be seen from dawn to dusk loping along. Several mega-races that attract thousands of runners are held along portions of the River Road during the summer. A small and companionable race, the Mom's Day Four-Mile is held each May on Mother's Day and begins at Riverside Park. Each finisher receives a potted plant.

If you're on the campus of the University of Minnesota anyway, begin your river run there, on the west bank campus. However, parking is so difficult on weekdays when the university is in session that if you've come to the river by car, you should park it at Riverside Park, or on the east side of the Franklin Avenue bridge, or on the west bank just off Ford Parkway, at the parking lot for the lock and dam.

If you're making a day of it with the family, begin your run and leave the non-runners at Minnehaha Park, where there are picnic tables, scenic vistas, and plenty of play equipment. Minnehaha Falls is here too, and a charming statue of Hiawatha and Minnehaha, the lovers made famous in Henry Wadsworth Longfellow's poem, *Hiawatha*. Longfellow never came near Minnesota — Harvard professors seldom did in those days — though a replica of his home stands, appropriately enough, at the intersection of Minnehaha Parkway and Hiawatha Avenue.

On the east bank, just opposite Riverside Park, and visible only from that bank, is the University Showboat, where 19th century melodramas are performed in the summer. Further south on East River Road, between Franklin and Marshall Avenues, is Eastcliff, the stately white mansion that is the home of the president of the University of Minnesota. These notable sights may be ignored, however, because the

River Road itself is one continuous scenic pleasure, shaded in summer, sheltered in winter, (except, of course, for the bridges, which can be cruel to cross as north winds funnel down the river gorge). If you tire of looking at river and wooded banks, you can turn your eyes to the elegant homes that line the River Road on both sides.

Most of the Mississippi River Road is flat. The area between Washington Avenue and Franklin, however, has hefty hills. The one, southbound, on the east bank, goes past the Variety Club Heart Hospital. This may be a comfort to you, knowing help is close at hand.

DISTANCE: Several loops are possible along the River Road.
    Minnehaha Park-Lake Street and return: 10K
    Minnehaha Park-Franklin and return: 15K
    Washington Bridge-Ford Parkway and return: 11 miles
    Washington Bridge to Lake Street and return: 10K
    Riverside Park-Lake-Franklin Bridge: 4 miles

BEGINNING POINTS: West Bank Campus (near Washington)
    Riverside Park
    Franklin and East River Road
    West River Road, just north of Ford Bridge
    Minnehaha Park, northeast corner.

DIFFICULTY: 1, except northernmost segment: 8

CONDITIONS:
    Aesthetics: 8
    Weather: No problem, except on bridges
    Traffic: No problem, asphalt paths
    Surface: Mostly asphalt; paths are better maintained on the Minneapolis than on the St. Paul segments. St. Paul has some gravelly, gullied areas. The Minneapolis side, from Ford Parkway to Lake Street, is very poorly lighted.

Minnehaha Parkway

MINNEHAHA PARKWAY

"The beautiful falls of Minnehaha are sufficiently celebrated. They do not need a lift from me in that direction."

Mark Twain, *Life on the Mississippi*

Minnehaha Parkway, which extends for several miles through south Minneapolis, is a magnificent place to run. It's always been a splendid resource in the heart of a great city, but until the late 1960's, the parkway's potential went unrealized. Then, under park superintendent Robert Ruhe, the entire city park system was revamped, and the parkway was developed into a multi-purpose recreational area. In the 1940's and 50's, Minnehaha Creek was a pleasant place to drive along on a Sunday afternoon. One saw an occasional child tossing pebbles into the water, or sailing a toy boat. Now, on any given summer Sunday you will see canoes and rubber rafts on the creek, pedestrians of all ages strolling along its banks, families picnicking at the designated areas, and runners.

In fact, the only drawback to running Minnehaha Parkway is that you will have plenty of company: small children, big dogs, backpackers-in-training, and all manner of foot traffic will be your companions. If you can avoid summer evenings and weekends, you'll have no complaints. You may have none even if you jog along during a high-density period. The natives are friendly. Almost everyone radiates the sense of having tremendous good fortune to be here at all.

A round trip from 36th Avenue to Lake Harriet and back, a distance of about 10 miles, includes three lakes and several attractive neighborhoods, but few places where you can get water or find toilet facilities. There is one oasis at Lynnhurst Field, just about at the halfway point, a gas station at Cedar Avenue, and possible resources at Lyndale — there's a public library branch just south of the parkway. If you've left a canteen of water in your car, you ought to get by without dehydrating except on the hottest days.

DISTANCE: about 10 miles

BEGINNING POINTS: 36th Avenue and Minnehaha Parkway or Lake Harriet and Minnehaha Parkway

DIFFICULTY: 3; some rolling hills, none significant

CONDITIONS:

Aesthetics: 6–10, improving as you go west.

Weather: Mostly shaded; a good cool place to run in summer. Not plowed in winter.

Traffic: No problem; most places, the running path is several yards from the street.

Surface: Asphalt

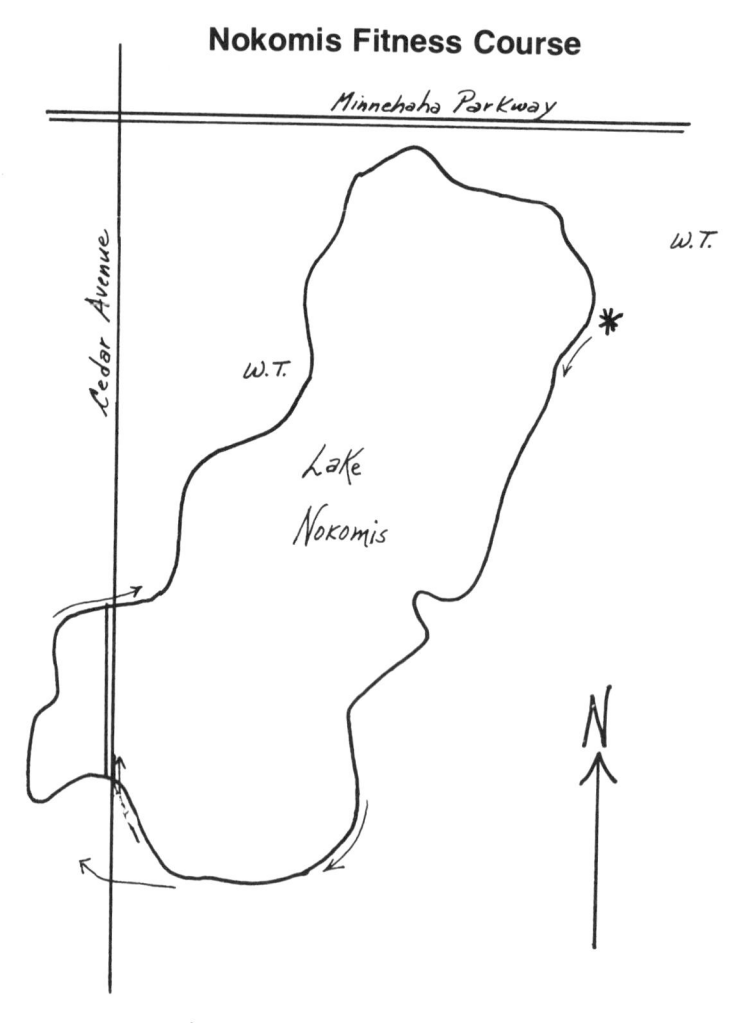

Nokomis Fitness Course

Minnehaha Parkway

Cedar Avenue

W.T.

W.T.

Lake Nokomis

N

If you are running the fitness course, follow the path to the Cedar Av. bridge and across. If not, cross Cedar south of the bridge.

NOKOMIS FITNESS RUN

What makes a run around Lake Nokomis memorable is its Vita Fitness Course. Patterned after a program developed in 1968 in Switzerland, the course consists of 20 stations placed around the lake. At each you are asked to perform a certain number of repetitions of a particular exercise. Some of these are the old favorites you remember from the Canadian Air Force Exercises that you gave up when you started running. Others are the unique contributions of the Swiss. You are the beneficiary of this international fitness conspiracy.

In truth, most of the exercises are fun. At one, you hang from rings and twist slowly in the wind. At another, you vault over a beam. At one of the last stations, you traverse a set of parallel bars. And at every station you will see a sign with a drawing of what you should look like as you perform the required activity. You must not permit yourself to be discouraged by these drawings.

The distance around the fitness course is about 2 miles; around all of Nokomis about 2½. If this is less than you are accustomed to running, the run is easily extendable either by repeating a circuit of the lake or by continuing along Minnehaha Parkway either to the east or to the west.

Water and toilets are available at the Nokomis Community Center, just up the hill from the beginning of the fitness course, or, in summer, at the beach, on the west shore of the lake. Picnic facilities are also abundant at Nokomis, and just across the parkway is Hiawatha Golf Course, a public facility.

DISTANCE: about 2½ miles, extendable

BEGINNING POINT: Parking lot on East Nokomis Parkway; run clockwise

DIFFICULTY: 1 for the run alone. It's perfectly flat.

CONDITIONS:
  Aesthetics: 8
  Weather: much of the course is shaded for summer comfort; it presents the usual problems of lakes in winter
  Traffic: no problem. You must cross Cedar Avenue twice, but traffic is regulated by stop lights.
  Surface: Asphalt

ST. PAUL RUNS

Downtown: Y–Lilydale

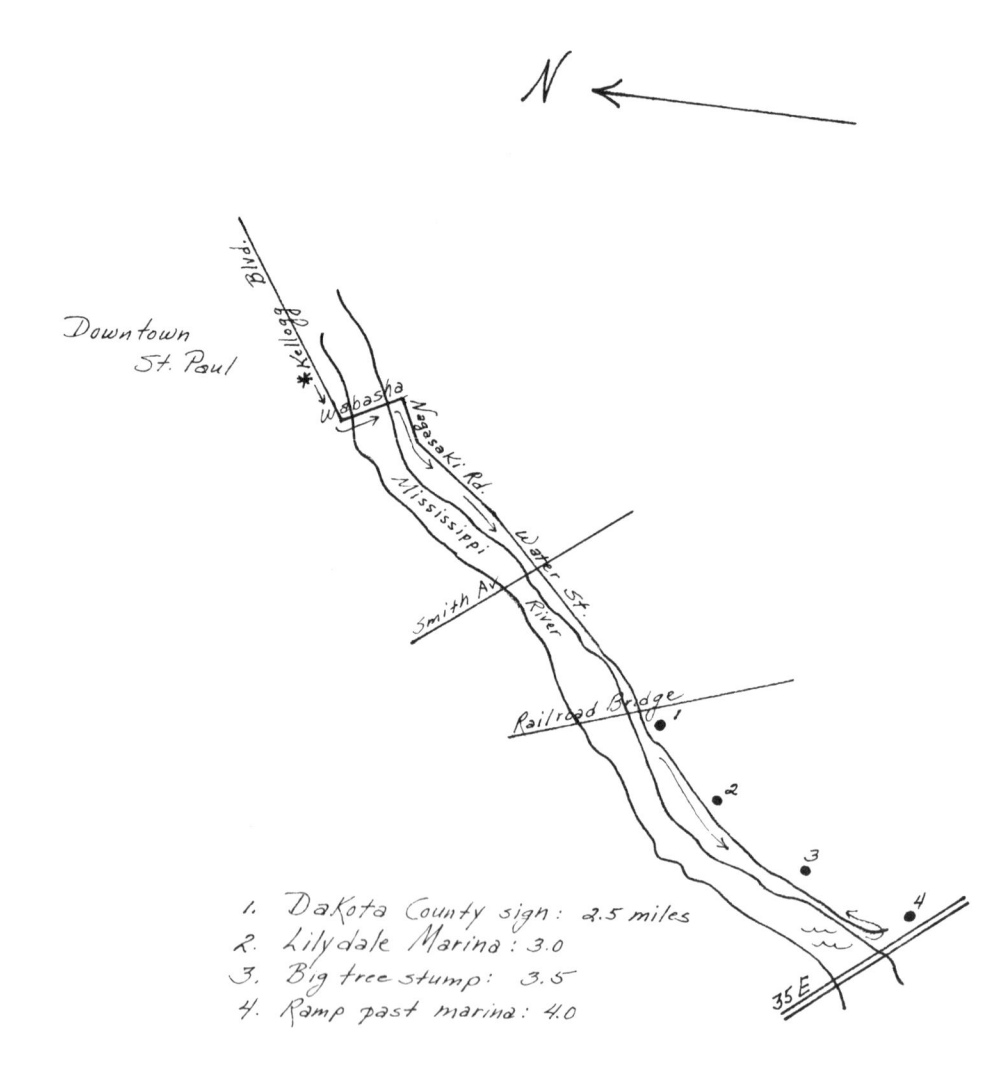

1. Dakota County sign: 2.5 miles
2. Lilydale Marina: 3.0
3. Big tree stump: 3.5
4. Ramp past marina: 4.0

DOWNTOWN YWCA TO LILYDALE

The finest downtown run in St. Paul is the route from the YWCA on Kellogg Boulevard to the Highway 35E bridge at Lilydale. The round trip is eight miles, but it's an out-and-back course, so you can modify the distance according to your time and zeal.

The Y provides locker and shower facilities for both men and women. For $.50 you may rent a locker; another $.25 buys the use of a towel.

Begin your run at the front door of the Y, run uphill to Wabasha, turn left, and cross the Wabasha Bridge. Just at the far end of the bridge, on your right, is Nagasaki Road (named for St. Paul's sister city in Japan). Run along Nagasaki until it merges into Water Street, and then continue to Lilydale. The charm of this route, which proceeds along the west bank of the Mississippi, is that after the first mile you are virtually in the country. The river is on your right; swamps, woods and impressive stone bluffs are on your left. True, you'll see an occasional pile of abandoned junk, and there's a shocking pink one-room schoolhouse along the way, but the overall atmosphere is very pleasant.

When you reach the sign that says you are entering Dakota County, you will have come 2.5 miles. The Lilydale Marina marks the three-mile distance; a large tree stump is at 3.5; and the end of the ramp which leads on from the next marina is 4 miles from where you started.

Although this route is fairly isolated, it is a favorite of noon-hour runners, so you are never alone for long.

DISTANCE: 8 miles

BEGINNING POINT: St. Paul YWCA, Kellogg Boulevard

DIFFICULTY: 2. Essentially flat except for Wabasha Bridge

CONDITIONS:

  Aesthetics: 6

  Weather: Shaded in summer for most of the route; gusty in winter, especially on return trip when the prevailing northwest winds come up the river.

  Traffic: Virtually none, although the route is along public roads.

  Surface: Asphalt mostly; cement for the few blocks leaving downtown St. Paul.

Women's History: Short Course

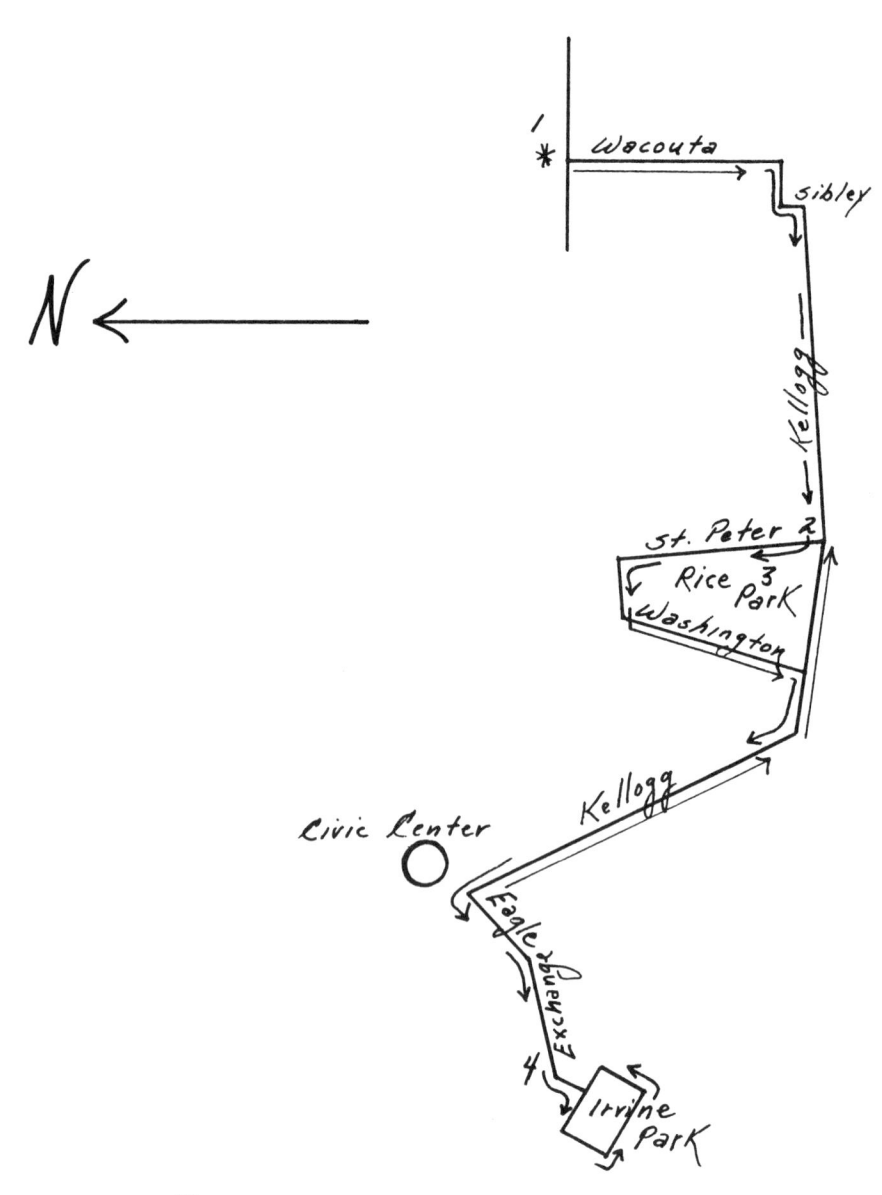

1. First Baptist Church
2. Minnesota Museum (formerly Women's City Club)
3. Rice Park: site of 1914 Suffrage Rally
4. Ramsey House

ST. PAUL WOMEN'S HISTORY: SHORT COURSE

If you work in downtown St. Paul or are staying at a downtown hotel, you can sample several sites significant to the history of women in this city.

A good place to begin is at the First Baptist Church, at the corner of 9th and Wacouta Streets. The church itself was founded in the 1840's by Harriet Bishop, the first white school-teacher in St. Paul. With becoming nineteenth-century modesty, she handed over the task of spiritual nurturance to the male clergy as soon as souls sufficient for a congregation had been gathered together. She taught the Sunday School. Her role in the educational and religious life of early St. Paul is commemorated in a scene on the front door of First Baptist today.

One of Harriet Bishop's social concerns, back in 1847, was temperance, and as you run down Wacouta Street toward Mears Park you will see that her battle is not yet won: victims of Demon Rum occasionally eye passing runners with mingled envy and suspicion.

Turn right onto 6th Street, then left onto Sibley, and follow Sibley to Kellogg Boulevard. Turn right onto Kellogg. You'll be running up hill for several blocks, and you'll pass the St. Paul YWCA, where water and toilets are available. At the corner of Kellogg and St. Peter Streets, you'll see the art deco facade of the Minnesota Museum of Art. The museum was originally the Women's City Club, designed "to provide for women a center for organized work and for social and intellectual intercourse." Amelia Earhart and Gertrude Stein were among the distinguished lecturers at the club in the 1930's. That the Club was built at all was due in large measure to the efforts of Alice O'Brien, philanthropists, world traveler, and art connoisseur who — among many other accomplishments — raised money for the building through an ingenious series of publicity stunts, including training her Great Dane dogs to deliver tickets held in their mouths to various city dignitaries.

Turn right onto St. Peter and proceed to 5th Street. Turn left, and then left again on Washington. This brief detour from Kellogg Boulevard will take you around Rice Park, site of a large women's suffrage rally in 1914.

Once back on Kellogg, proceed on to the Civic Center, at which you must cross the street and run down Eagle Street to Exchange. At the corner of Walnut and Exchange is the Italianate edifice, the Ramsey

House, residence of Minnesota's first governor, Alexander Ramsey. From here, turn left and run down and around Irvine Park, where the homes once owned by St. Paul's elite families are being restored to their former splendor. Both the Ramsey House and the houses of Irvine Park are evocative of that period in nineteenth century America when the ideals of True Womanhood prevailed. Inside her mansion, elegant at least by the standards of pioneer Minnesota, Anna Ramsey poured tea, received guests, and talked about nothing of substance. That she ever went running, or even briskly walking, is unthinkable. Merely ascending a flight of stairs was probably exercise enough for a True Woman, especially when belted and corsetted according to the fashions of the day, and draped in about fifteen pounds of skirts.

From here you may simply retrace your steps back to downtown St. Paul.

DISTANCE: About 3.5 miles

BEGINNING POINT: First Baptist; 9th & Wacouta

DIFFICULTY: 4

CONDITIONS:

    Aesthetics: 1, except for Irvine Park, whose restored Victorian charm rates at least a 5.

    Weather: No special problems

    Traffic: Regulated by stop lights, which will slow you down some.

    Surface: Cement sidewalks

Cass Gilbert Run

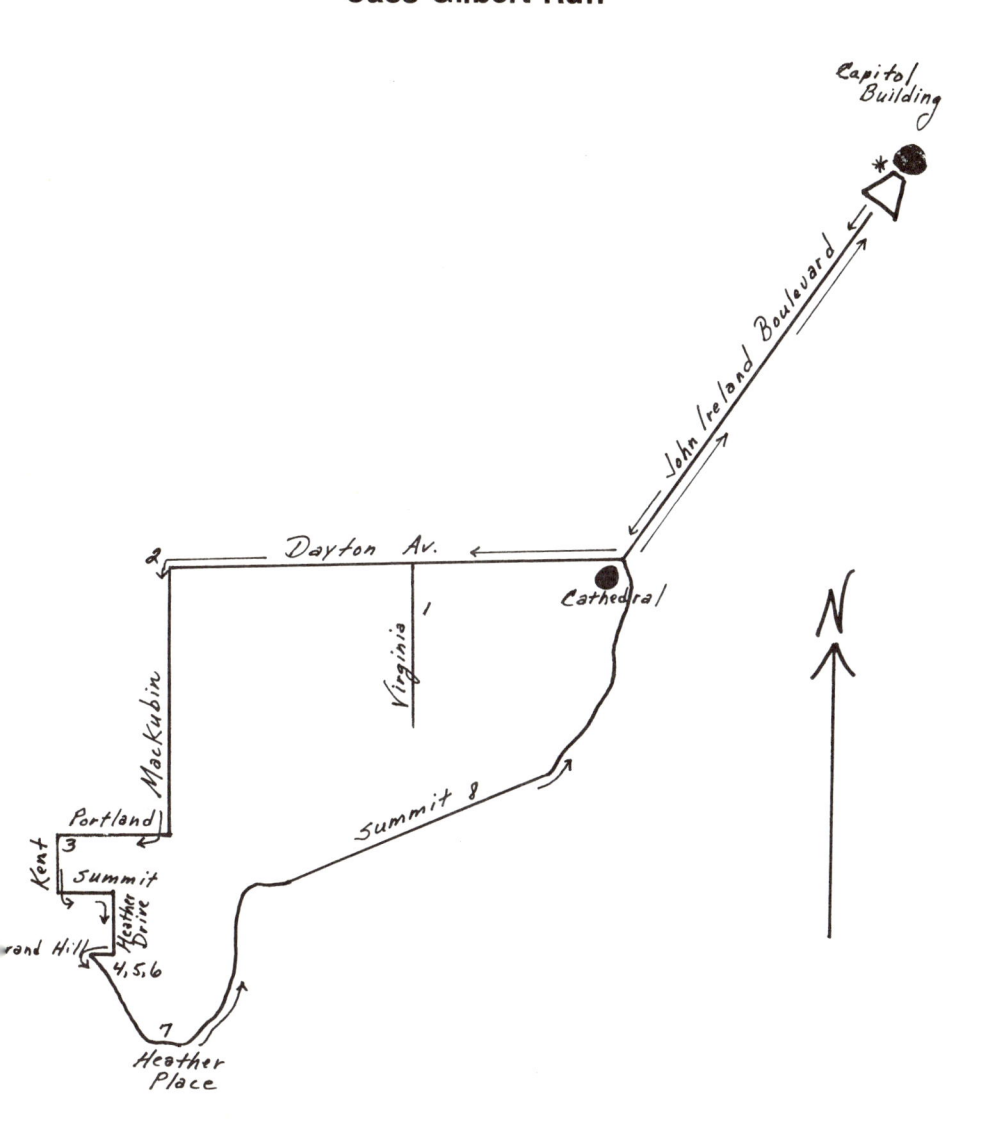

1. Virginia Avenue Church
2. Dayton Avenue Presbyterian
3. Row houses, 548-554 Portland
4. Residence, 520 Grand Hill
5. Residence, 514 Grand Hill
6. Residence, 506 Grand Hill
7. Gilbert House, 1 Heather Place
8. Lightner House, 318 Summit

CASS GILBERT RUN: CAPITOL-SUMMIT

If you're a lunch-hour runner who works in the state capitol area, you can have a good workout and an interesting run by tracing some of the architectural work of Cass Gilbert. Gilbert was Minnesota's chief exponent of the City Beautiful movement of the late nineteenth and early twentieth centuries — the pictorial tradition of the grand boulevard, axial streets, circles and squares, and monumental public buildings. His most characteristic work is the state capitol itself and the entire capitol approach area, but he designed private homes, churches, and apartment blocks as well as public buildings.

This run, in addition to taking you past Gilbert buildings and other structures of St. Paul's rich and elegant founding fathers, will give you a clear idea of why Summit Avenue was so named: a substantial hill awaits your ascent as you leave the capitol approach.

Begin at the foot of the capitol steps and run straight toward the Cathedral — you can't miss it! — along John Ireland Boulevard, named for the man who for 34 years was Roman Catholic Archbishop of St. Paul. Ireland, born in — you guessed it — Ireland, was a fighting chaplain in the Civil War and then returned to St. Paul where he became an important figure in both the religious and civic life of the city. He was responsible for the building of the Cathedral, and for establishing the College of St. Thomas and the St. Paul Seminary. His sister, Seraphina Ireland, founded the College of St. Catherine.

Proceed on Ireland Boulevard to Dayton Avenue, the street that is on the north side of the Cathedral, about .6 of a mile from the capitol. Turn right on Dayton and run up to Mackubin. Three blocks before Mackubin you will come to Virginia Avenue. Look to your left and you'll see, a block or two south, a small Cass Gilbert church, built in 1896, at 170 Virginia. You can either detour south for a closer look — it's well worth it — or continue along Dayton where, at the corner of Dayton and Mackubin you'll see a massive Romanesque Gilbert church of reddish stone, the Dayton Avenue Presbyterian, built at the same time as its neighbor on Virginia.

Turn left onto Mackubin, continue until you reach Portland, then turn right on Portland and go one block west to Kent. On the southeast corner, 548-554 Portland, is a series of brick row houses with dark shutters and bays, designed by Gilbert and built in 1888. It's a handsome structure.

Turn left onto Kent, then left again onto Summit, and right onto Heather Drive. (Incidentally, in 1917-18 Sinclair Lewis lived at 516 Summit, the corner of Summit and Heather Drive, while trying to write a novel about James J. Hill which he never finished.) Continue on Heather Drive to Grand Hill, where you can see, at 506, 514, and 520, three houses designed by Gilbert at the turn of the century and distinguished chiefly by their dissimilarity from one another.

You have probably figured out by now that Gilbert designed houses in a variety of styles. His own house, at 1 Heather Place, combines the English Queen Anne style with influences of the Arts and Crafts movement. The Gilbert House may be reached by turning right onto Grand Hill, then jogging immediately left onto Heather Place and following the street as it curves around to your left. One Heather Place is on your left.

Follow the street back to Summit, turn right onto Summit and continue back toward the capitol, pausing to note the fine Romanesque-styled Lightner House, designed by Cass Gilbert and built in 1896, at 318 Summit.

From here on it's downhill past the cathedral as Summit merges into John Ireland Boulevard again and takes you back to the capitol approach area.

DISTANCE: 3.6 miles

BEGINNING POINT: State capitol building

DIFFICULTY: 5

CONDITIONS:

  Aesthetics: 5

  Weather: Course is mostly shaded and residential, providing shelter from winter wind and summer sun. Only exception is the first and last half mile.

  Traffic: No problem; run on sidewalks

  Surface: Cement

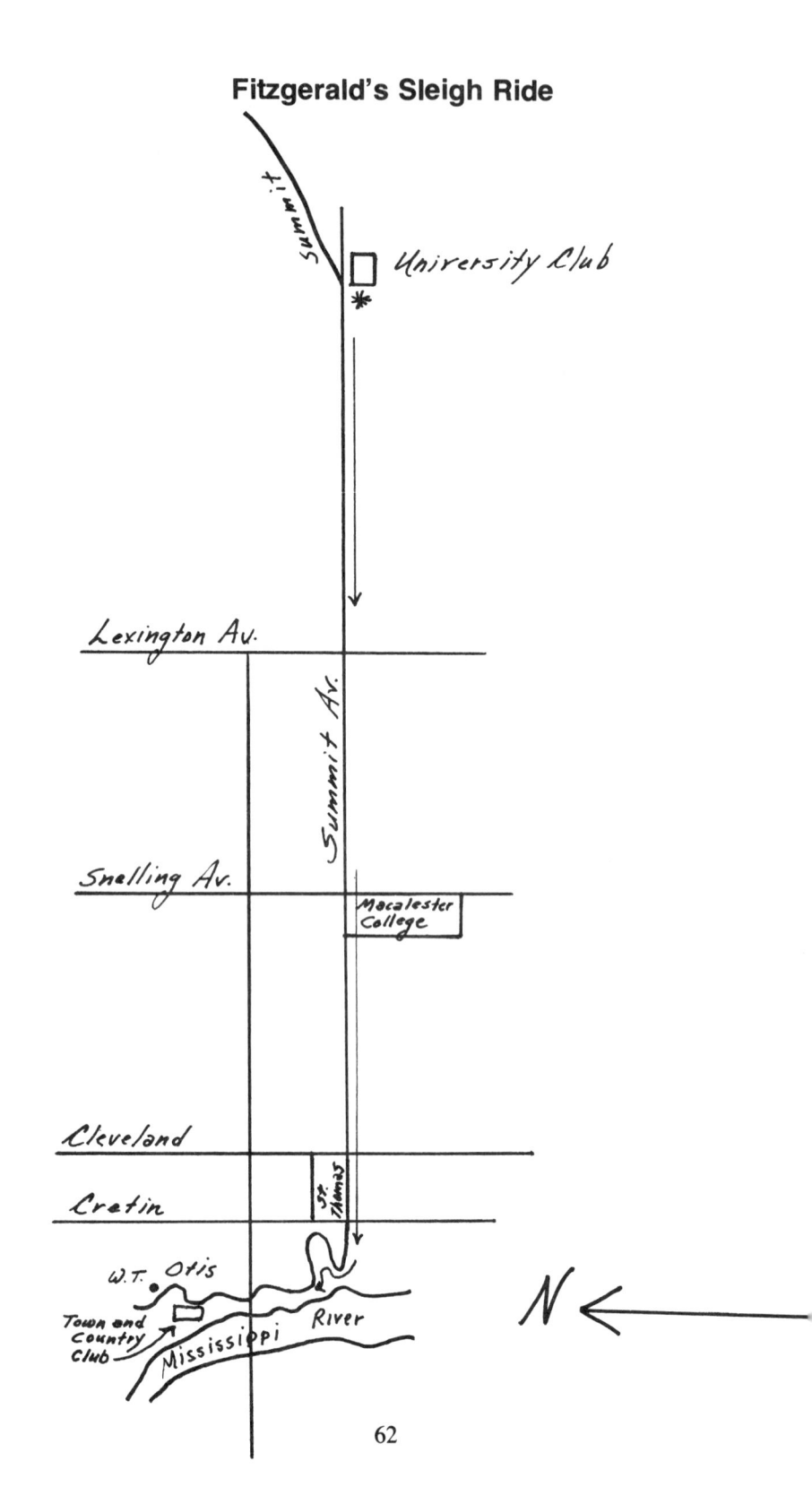

Fitzgerald's Sleigh Ride

FITZGERALD'S SLEIGH RIDE

Summit Avenue, a favorite of many runners, is the locale of many buildings sacred to the memory of writer F. Scott Fitzgerald. One such site is marked with an historic plaque: the row house at 599 Summit where, in 1919, Fitzgerald completed his first novel, *This Side of Paradise*.

Although Fitzgerald never attained any distinction as a runner, it is said that when he received word from Scribner's that his novel had been accepted for publication, he ran up and down Summit, stopping cars and telling friends and casual acquaintances the good news.

Two of his haunts are useful destinations for runners: the University Club at Summit and Ramsey hill, and the Town and Country Club, just off Marshall Avenue and the River Road. The route is one Fitzgerald always remembered fondly as one down which he'd gone on many jolly sleighrides. The Town and Country Club is the place where he allegedly met his first love, Ginevra King.

The round trip, from the University Club to Town and Country and back again, is ten miles. West of Lexington Avenue, you can run down the center of the tree-shaded (where Dutch Elm disease has not yet struck) boulevard to the River Road, run briefly up the River Road to Marshall, then up Marshall to Otis and the T & C.

Bill Rodgers himself could die of dehydration on the steps of the Town and Country if not a member, but the Halfway House, half a block north and just inside the entrance to the golf course, has a drinking fountain. It also has a soft drink-snack bar that you can patronize if you are not intimidated by the sniffish looks of the golfers.

On your way along Summit you will pass Macalester College, at Snelling, and St. Thomas College, between Cleveland and Cretin. A little rummaging around at either of these places will turn up water and toilet facilities.

When you're finished with your run, you may want to stop at Kardamena's Cafe, a vegetarian natural-foods restaurant at 364 Selby near Western. It's in the old Dakotah Building, site of W. A. Frost's Pharmacy, where Scott used to drop in for a coke and conversation.

DISTANCE: 10 miles

BEGINNING POINT: University Club at Summit and Ramsey

DIFFICULTY: 1; flat course, 1 small hill

CONDITIONS:

Aesthetics: 8 — urban. Summit Avenue has been called the best-preserved Victorian boulevard in the United States.

Weather: Runnable either winter or summer. T & C halfway house not open in winter.

Traffic: No problem, if you stick to the sidewalk and to the center of the boulevard west of Lexington.

Surface: Cement, packed earth, asphalt

Transportation: The MTC bus runs on Grand Avenue, just one block south of Summit, and on Marshall and Selby.

Cherokee Heights

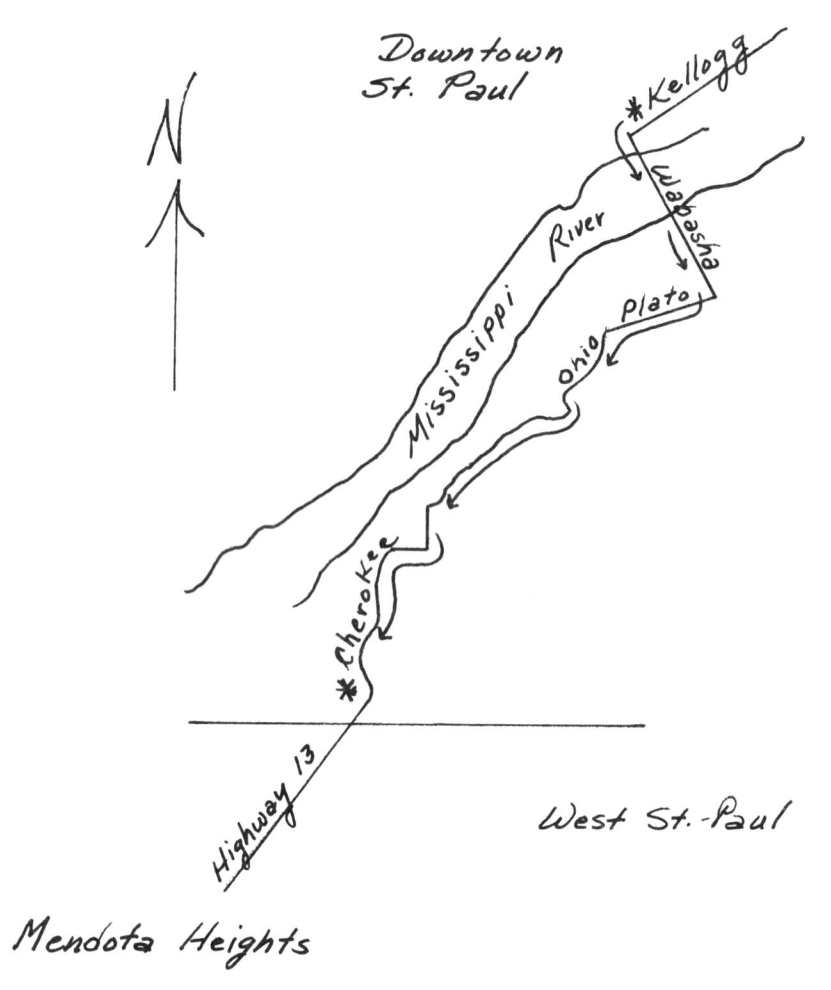

CHEROKEE HEIGHTS

A hilly, scenic, 2½ mile run begins and ends in Cherokee Park where there are toilet facilities, parking, water, picnic tables, and children's play equipment. The run provides striking vistas of the Mississippi River and of downtown St. Paul. Some of the Heights area is wooded, some of it is residential. The hills are formidable.

One of the attractions of Cherokee Heights is that it is easily reached from downtown St. Paul. If you're driving from downtown to reach the starting point of this run, cross the Wabasha Bridge, take Wabasha to Plato Boulevard, turn right onto Plato, then left onto Ohio Street, and follow Ohio up to the Heights and on to the Park itself, which is about 1¼ miles from the intersection of Plato and Ohio.

Runners who work downtown and can stretch a lunch hour a tad, or who are from out of town and staying at a midtown hotel, can simply run the distance.

If you happen to be in charge of some small children, the play equipment in Cherokee Park is good, varied, and fairly tame. Also, there are no precipices from which children are likely to tumble while their parent(s) is/are putting in their mileage.

You can also extend this run southward into Mendota Heights along Highway 13, which is variously called the Sioux Trail and Sibley Memorial Highway — depending, apparently, upon the inclinations of the mapmakers and signposters. The shoulders of Highway 13 are very narrow, however, and there are several blind curves on steep hills. Traffic can be a problem.

DISTANCE: 2½ miles, extendable; from downtown St. Paul

BEGINNING POINT: Parking lot in Cherokee Park, or corner of Kellogg and Wabasha

DIFFICULTY: 8

CONDITIONS:

Aesthetics: 8 for Cherokee Park; 3 for downtown-Cherokee segment

Weather: Windy in winter on the Heights and crossing river

Traffic: No special problems; sidewalks available, except if extended along Highway 13 southbound.

Surface: cement and asphalt

Edgcumbe-Highland

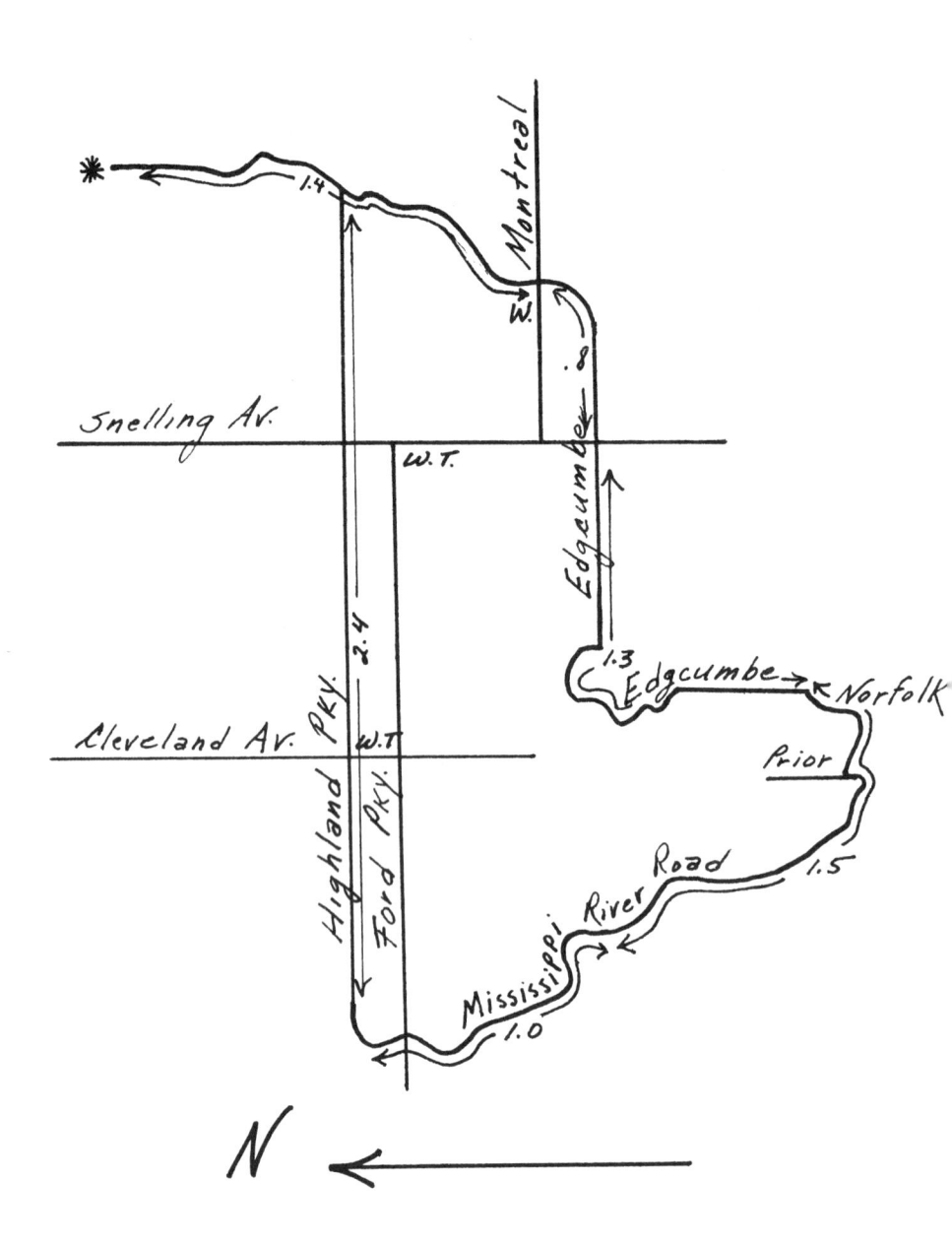

EDGCUMBE-HIGHLAND-RIVER ROAD

This is an appealing run that takes you through one of the nicest neighborhoods in St. Paul, up and down some impressive hills, and along a scenic stretch of the Mississippi. Its only limitations are a paucity of water and toilet facilities, and a brief stretch of potentially troublesome traffic.

Begin at Jefferson and Edgcumbe, and run south along the boulevard to Montreal. Here, at the edge of the Highland golf course, on the southwest corner of Edgcumbe and Montreal there is a drinking fountain; you might miss it, because it is on the opposite side of a plaque commemorating the city fathers who made this public golf course possible. You might not care if you miss it, because it is less than a mile and a half from your start.

Continue along Edgcumbe as it turns east along the south side of the park. After another two miles, the parkway swings southward again and steeply downhill. This is the one segment where there is neither sidewalk nor boulevard to run on, and there is a blind curve that makes it desirable and safer for you to run WITH rather than opposite the traffic. Just when you think that you're abut to enter the freeway, your course jogs to the right and then quickly to the left again, along Norfolk Avenue. From Norfolk you have a fine view of some noteworthy sites: Fort Snelling, Mendota Bridge, and the landing approach for the Twin Cities International Airport.

Turn left onto Prior, and in a short block you will reach the Mississippi River Road, where an asphalt path is before you. About two miles of running along the river road brings you past the Ford Motor Company Assembly Plant, and just beyond the Ford Bridge. Turn right onto Highland Parkway and begin a long uphill climb to Snelling Avenue. By now you may be longing for a drop of water. There are possibilities at gas stations on Cleveland and Highland, but they're not always open on weekends. If all else fails, when you reach Snelling, turn right and take a one-block detour to the corner of Snelling and Ford Parkway. A dependable all-hours gas station is on the southwest corner.

Back on your appointed course, it's mostly downhill from Snelling to Edgcumbe, and then along Edgcumbe to your starting point.

DISTANCE: 9½ miles

BEGINNING POINT: Jefferson and Edgcumbe

DIFFICULTY: 7 (long uphill on Highland Parkway)

CONDITIONS:

Aesthetics: 8

Weather: Much of the run is shaded and residential. The 2-mile river road stretch is due north: can be nasty in winter.

Traffic: No problem, except for brief stretch before Norfolk

Surface: Cement, asphalt, or, if you choose, grass for much of the way

St. Anthony Park

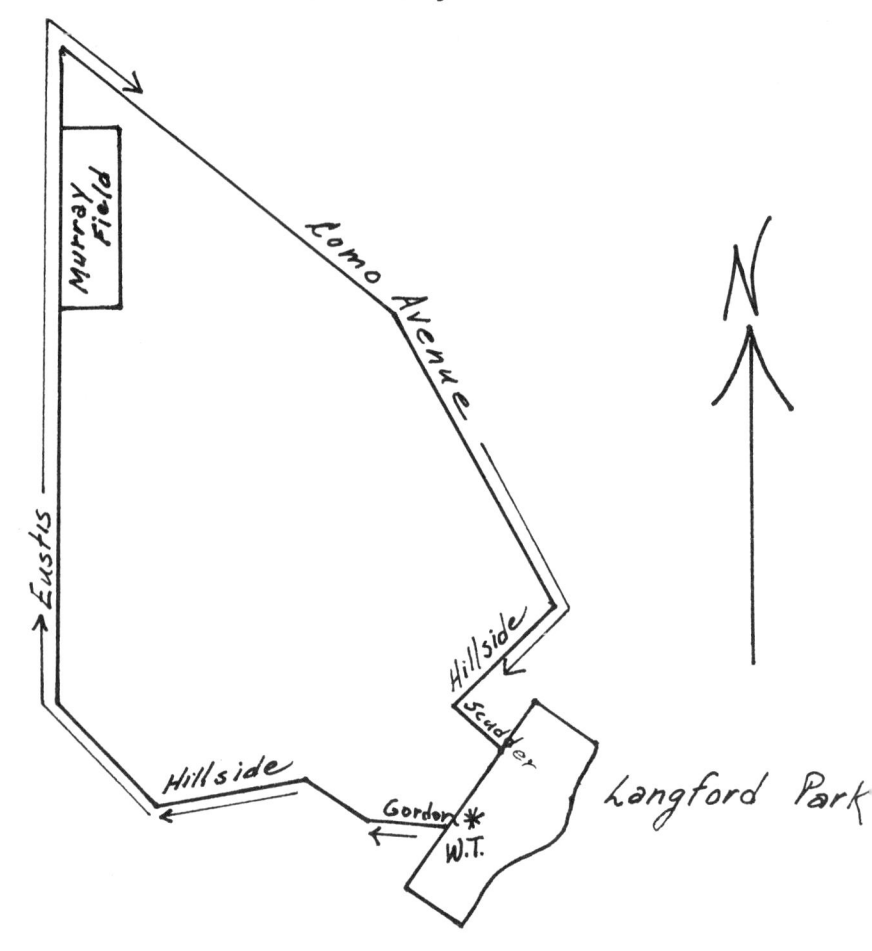

ST. ANTHONY PARK-UNIVERSITY GROVE

St. Anthony Park is the St. Paul neighborhood that is nearest to Minneapolis. It is also near the fairgrounds, the St. Paul campus of the University of Minnesota, two golf courses, and an architecturally-interesting neighborhood.

The neighborhood is the University Grove, land owned by the University of Minnesota and set aside in 1928 by the Board of Regents as an area where tenured faculty members could lease lots and build their own homes. The prospective homeowner must engage an architect whose plans, in turn, must meet certain specifications laid down by the university. If a house is sold, it must be sold to another tenured faculty member. Many interesting architectural styles and land-use ideas may be seen in The Grove, as neighbors call it, — so many, in fact, that only a few highlights can be absorbed on a single run.

One land-use concept easily seen in The Grove is the Superblock. Originally a European idea, and one promoted by Lewis Mumford and used by Clarence Stein in New Jersey, New York, and the Greenbelt Towns of the 1930's, the superblock provides green play spaces — not streets or alleys — in the center of each block. Pathways connect residents with these open areas.

The St. Anthony Park area also has a number of structures of interest. The community was planned in the early 1870's by the landscape architect Horace Cleveland. He designed curvilinear streets and preserved the irregular terrain of the site. Some homes of this earliest period of building remain: for example, at 2203 Scudder is the 1880's home of Governor Andrew McGill. Most homes in The Park were built between 1900–1920, however, and represent a variety of styles.

For the runner, this area has several attractions: hills, a measured running track, and Muffuletta's, a restaurant with some vegetarian entrees and a good Sunday brunch. Although you could work out several St. Anthony Park-Grove runs, the one given here is a two-mile course over which low-key neighborhood races take place on July 4 and Winter Sports Day in February.

Bus service is available on Como Avenue and goes to both Minneapolis and St. Paul.

DISTANCE: 2 miles for the race route.

BEGINNING POINT: Langford Park

DIFFICULTY: 6

CONDITIONS:

Aesthetics: 5

Weather: Mostly shaded from summer sun, except along westernmost stretch. This same unprotected stretch is subject to strong winter winds out of the northwest.

Traffic: The part of the route that must be run in the street does not have much traffic. Be careful on hillcrests, however,

Surface: Asphalt and cement sidewalks.

COLISEUM

One of the few public indoor running tracks is located in the Coliseum on the state fairgrounds. Between 11:30 a.m. and 1 p.m. Monday through Fridays in the winter, the Coliseum is open to both skaters and runners. Runners use a 1/5 mile cement track. Admission is $1. There are shower facilities and pegs on which to hang your clothes, but no lockers and no place to leave valuables. The addition of sandwich and beverage service is planned for 1980.

Cement is hard on the joints, so you probably won't want to do all your mileage here, but frozen ground isn't much better, and the absence of a wind-chill factor will probably compensate for any extra aches and pains you may feel after a long run at the Coliseum.

Indoor tracks exist at most of the Twin Cities colleges, at the University of Minnesota, the Athletic Clubs and at the Y's. Most of these are membership-only facilities, and they are much smaller than the Coliseum's track, and thus require far more circuits per mile.

The Coliseum is on Como Avenue, about ¼ mile west of Snelling Avenue on the fairgrounds.

Lake Como

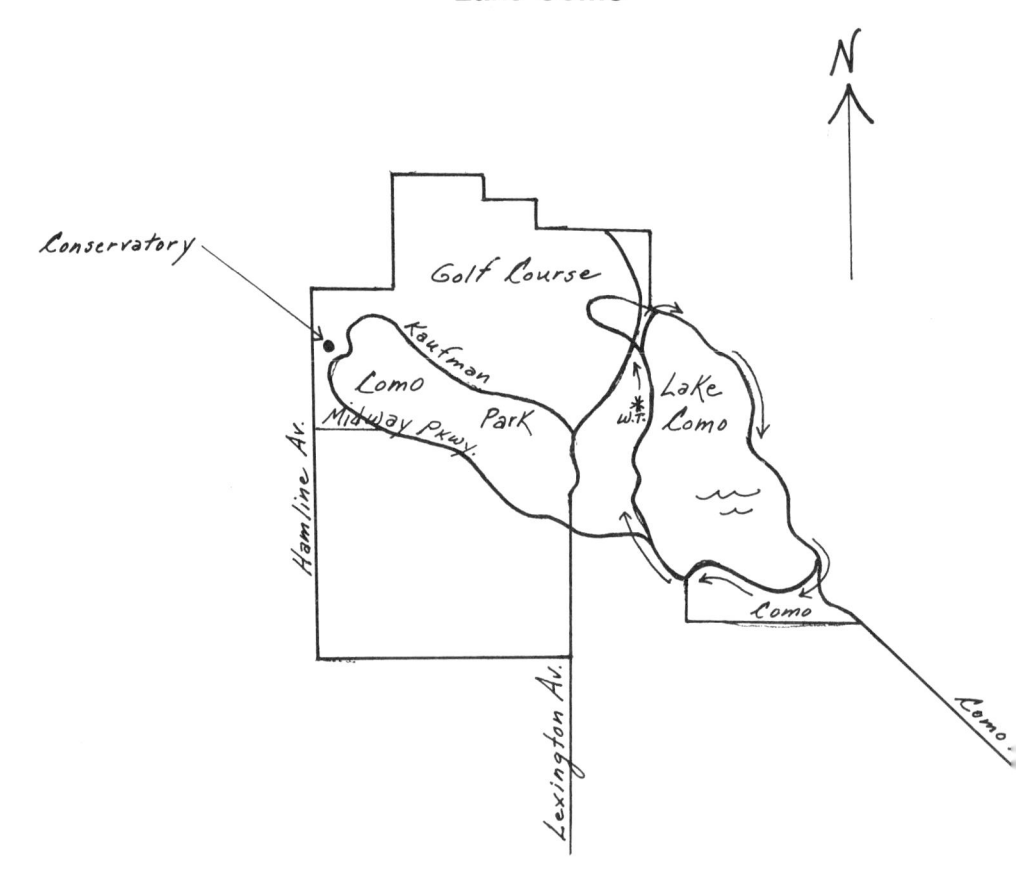

COMO

Lake Como has several attractions. First of all, it is exactly 1 2/3 miles around. Thus three circuits is a tidy five miles, six circuits ten. Secondly, there is water, phone, toilets, and shelter at the pavilion on the west side. Thirdly, there is always a great variety of interesting activities taking place around Como, some scheduled, some not. For example, the parking lot just south of the pavilion is an American-Graffiti-style rutting ground for hot rodders and vanners. On almost any warm evening, from April through October, one can observe an impressive display of metal, chrome, and contemporary mating customs. Other attractions include the speed-skating races in January during the St. Paul winter carnival, band concerts on summer evenings, and church services on Sunday mornings.

Spring, that climatic change that occurs here briefly sometime in May, is wonderful anywhere in the Twin Cities, but especially at Lake Como. Ducks of all sorts abound on the lake, and vast broods of ducklings can be seen in convoy. Spring warblers seem particularly to like the small trees along the lakeshore, and many varieties are abundant there during their annual transit northward.

A final attraction, of course, is that the lake adjoins a large park which includes a zoo, a conservatory (it would be more aptly called a botanical garden), and a fine public golf course.

An excellent late-winter restorative is a visit to the conservatory's tropical climes after a run in the bitter cold. If you're discreet, you can picnic among the palm trees and waterfalls.

DISTANCE: 1⅔, extendable

BEGINNING POINT: Parking lot by pavilion on west side of lake.

DIFFICULTY: 1

CONDITIONS:

  Aesthetics: 6

  Weather: The running path is excellently maintained in winter. It is plowed to the asphalt quickly after each snowfall — much better than Lake of the Isles, for example, in Minneapolis.

  Traffic: Path is shared with bikers — not divided as around Minneapolis lakes — and bicycle traffic can be heavy on summer evenings and weekends.

  Surface: Asphalt

Wheelock Parkway

WHEELOCK PARKWAY

Improbable as it may seem, Minnesota was once touted as a haven for the health-seeker. It seems to fly in the face of common sense! A century and more ago, Minnesota boosters claimed that the climate here could cure a wide variety of ills. The claim was difficult to disprove: if you died of your chronic ailment after you got here, perhaps you'd simply waited too long to come!

Joseph Wheelock was one of the lucky ones. He came in 1850 to improve his health, founded the *St. Paul Pioneer Press* in 1861, and much later became president of the St. Paul Board. After his death at the age of 75, the parkway was named in his honor to commemorate his efforts to complete the St. Paul park system.

You can leave your car on the east side of Lake Como, just opposite the pavilion, and begin your run by going south along the lake for about .4 of a mile until you reach Wheelock Parkway. Turn left onto the parkway and follow it for its nearly five-mile length. You will enter the Phalen Park area just after you cross Arcade Street, the park's western border. Continue on to Phalen Drive, the entrance to which is marked by fieldstone pillars. You will come to the Phalen beach house, where there is water and toilet facilities — if the weather is nice. If you want to add a circuit of Lake Phalen (three miles) and then head back to Lake Como, you will have completed just over a half-marathon.

The route is mostly flat, except where the parkway descends down the bluff about two miles from Lake Como, and where it ascends sharply east of the overpass over Highway 35E. These are formidable hills — especially westbound on the return trip.

Wheelock Parkway runs through residential areas for much of its length and crosses some fairly busy intersections (regulated with traffic lights) where the desperate runner could find water or bathroom in a pinch. There is a splendid gas station just east of 35E on Wheelock, with elegant toilet facilities. Even in the gas-starved summer of 1979 it was open on weekends.

This parkway is considerably less isolated than some stretches of the West River Road or Minnehaha Parkway in Minneapolis.

DISTANCE: 10.6, Como to Phalen and return; 13.6 if circuit of Lake Phalen is included.

BEGINNING POINT: Parking lot, Como Boulevard, east side of Lake Como opposite pavilion.

DIFFICULTY: 5

CONDITIONS:

Aesthetics: 5

Weather: Course is mostly shaded and residential, providing shelter from winter wind and summer sun. Some short unprotected stretches are likely to be gusty in winter, hot in summer. In winter, some strectches have to be run in the street.

Traffic: Light. In summer, all of the route can be run off the streets, on boulevards or sidewalks.

Surface: Asphalt, cement, grass

Lake Phalen

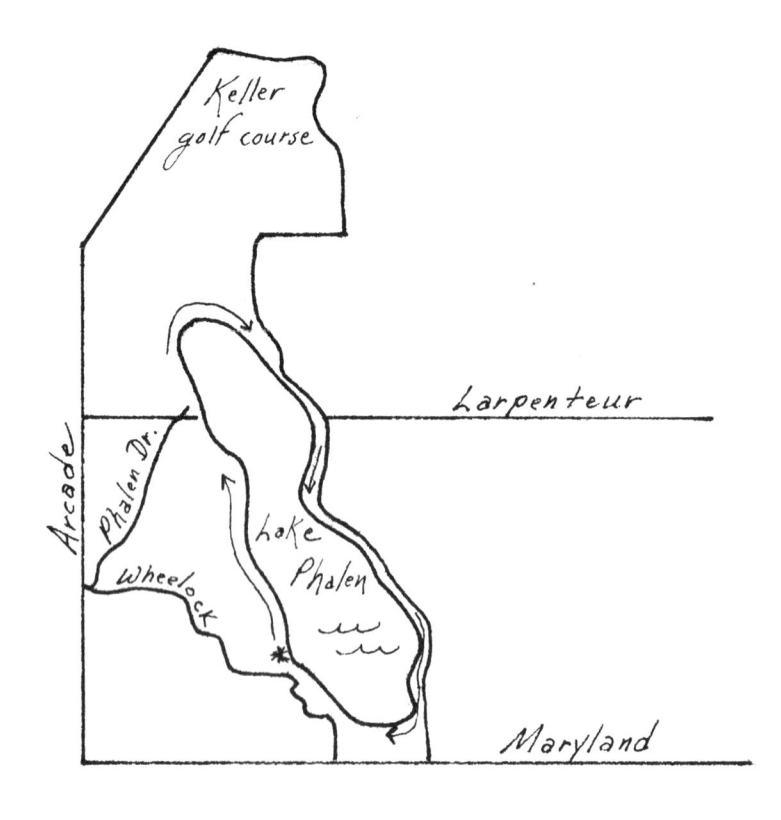

LAKE PHALEN

Lake Phalen is located in the northeastern corner of St. Paul, and it is connected by parkways to Indian Mounds Park on the south and to Como Park on the west. Like Lake Calhoun in Minneapolis, it is 3.1 miles (5 Kilometers) in circumference and therefore is suitable for training at popular racing distances. On the east shore of Lake Phalen, at Larpenteur, the Countryside Bicycle Trail to Stillwater begins. If you're feeling in a marathoning mood, this provides a scenic, hilly trip of 20-odd miles past several lakes, on side roads, some of which are unpaved. If you're thinking of something slightly less ambitious, you may wish to extend your run from the north end of Lake Phalen over to Keller Lake, which is less than a mile away.

There is a fine beach at the south end of Lake Phalen, and a golf course right across the street.

DISTANCE: One circuit of Phalen is 3.1 miles.

BEGINNING POINT: Beach area parking lot at south end of lake on Phalen Drive, just north of Wheelock Parkway.

DIFFICULTY: 2–3

CONDITIONS:
  Aesthetics: 7
  Weather: Shaded from summer sun; gusty in winter
  Traffic: No problem. Running path is separated from street
  Surface: Asphalt

Johnson Parkway

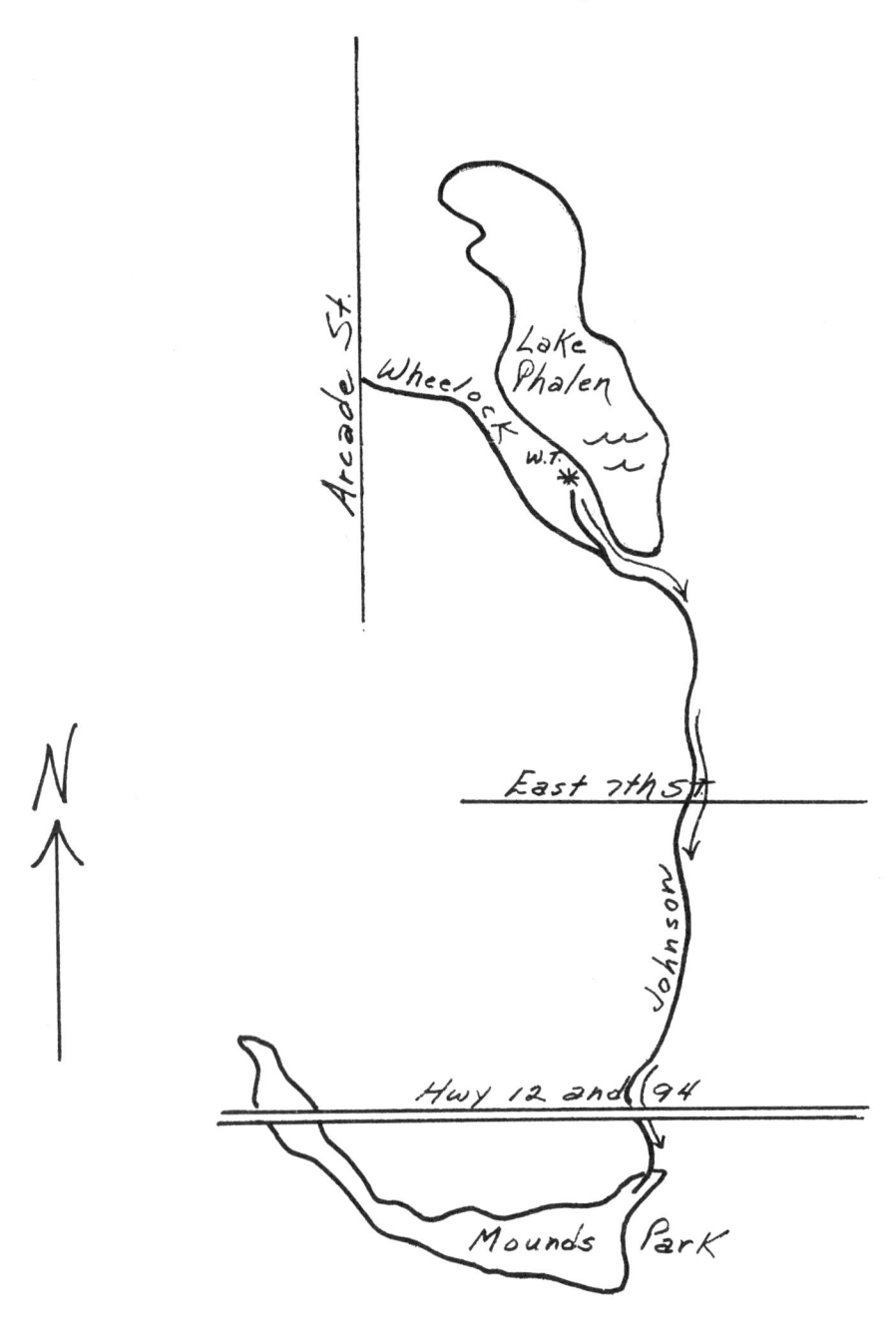

JOHNSON PARKWAY

In most cities, Johnson Parkway, running nearly the full length of the east side of St. Paul, and connecting two recreational areas, would be considered an urban treasure. By comparison with the more elegant and scenic Minnehaha Parkway in Minneapolis, however, it may seem dowdy. Among Johnson's advantages to the runner is the fact that it is *not* overrun — with bikers, roller skaters, or strollers.

Johnson Parkway connects Lake Phalen and Indian Mounds Park. You can leave your car on the west side of Lake Phalen, near the beach house just off Phalen Drive. The sign says, "Parking for Swimmers and Joggers Only." Begin your run by going south and following Phalen Drive around until it meets Johnson Parkway. Turn right onto Johnson and follow it for about 2½ miles. The parkway ends at Burns, which in turn jogs over to Mounds Parkway — turn right — which takes you to the top of the bluff and to the prehistoric Indian mounds. Water and toilet facilities are available in the picnic grounds at Mounds Park and at the beach house at Phalen — but don't count on them if it's raining. Only Lake Como's facilities seem to be "all weather" in St. Paul.

The parkway itself is fairly flat until you near the Indian Mounds area. Then it rises steeply to the top of Dayton's Bluff, where the mounds and the park are located.

DISTANCE: 6½ miles round trip

BEGINNING POINT: Beach house parking lot at Lake Phalen

DIFFICULTY: 5

CONDITIONS:
   Aesthetics: 5
   Weather: Most of the parkway is shaded against summer sun, and because the route goes through residential areas, the winter wind doesn't get a terrific sweep, except in a few places.
   Traffic: Most of this run is off the street, so traffic isn't a problem.
   Surface: Asphalt, cement, and some stretches of grass which must be run in the street in winter.

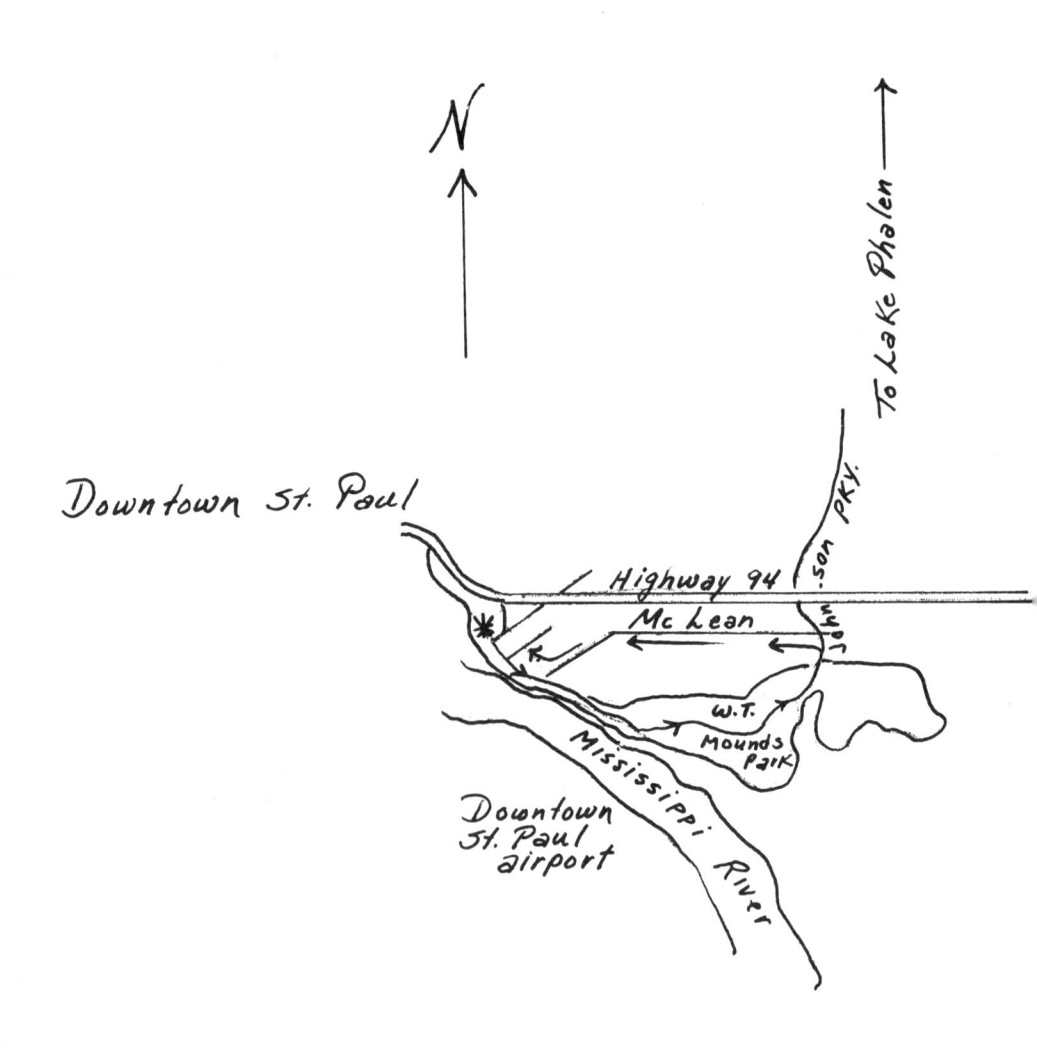

MOUNDS PARK

MOUNDS PARK

Mounds Park offers good views, good hills, and interesting evidence of both historic and prehistoric Minnesota. It is located atop Dayton's Bluff, which was named after Lyman Dayton, a leading real estate speculator of early St. Paul. Mr. Dayton, it is written, weighed 300 pounds, wore a long coat, velvet vest with white embroidery, and a huge watch chain, and was nicknamed "Sonny." He was apparently a quarrelsome man, sometimes beating his mother and once arrested for assault with a pistol. Perhaps running would have trimmed his girth, calmed his temper, and extended his lifespan. Alas, he died at 55 in 1865, too soon to capitalize on the real estate boom of the 1870's, which would have made him a very wealthy man.

You can begin this run on Mounds Boulevard, parking at the plaque marking the now-vanished Carver's Cave. (Mounds Boulevard is easily accessible from Highway 94 eastbound from downtown St. Paul.) The asphalt and then cement walkway rises rapidly to the top of the bluff after about 1/2 mile. At the top you will see the Indian Mounds for which the park is named, and if you turn right, into the traffic circle, and jog through it, you will have a splendid view of the Mississippi and downtown St. Paul. A plaque will help explain what you are seeing: the entire riverbed of the prehistoric River Warren, which once occupied the lowlands. At the base of Dayton's Bluff once ran the wagon and ox cart trails that took pioneers into St. Paul and further north and west into the Red River Valley and beyond.

Across from the Indian mounds is a spacious picnic area with water and toilets available. Continue on Mounds Boulevard to Johnson Parkway. Turn left onto Johnson, run down Johnson to McLean, turn left on McLean and follow it back to Mounds Boulevard. Turn right, continue your run another block or two, and you will be back at the parking lot.

DISTANCE: 2½ miles

BEGINNING POINT: Parking lot off Mounds Park Boulevard at Cherry

DIFFICULTY: 6

CONDITIONS:

   Aesthetics: First half 7; second half 3

   Weather: In winter, winds a problem for the first mile; water and toilets not available in winter. In summer, much of the course is shaded.

   Traffic: Light. Most of this run is on asphalt walking paths or cement sidewalk.

   Surface: Asphalt and cement

RESTAURANTS

Runners don't need special places to eat, but they are likely to scorn the fast-food burger factories in favor of vegetarian or natural foods restaurants. There are several of these in the Twin Cities area, and more seem to be sprouting up all the time. Some forbid smoking entirely within their premises. Some offer bulletin boards on which one can find notices of yoga classes for runners and wilderness trips for women, or haiku poetry contributed by inspired diners.

Most of the veggie restaurants happen to be near areas where there's good running too, so if you and your fellow-runners subscribe to Dr. George Sheehan's theory about the sweat of honest toil being inoffensive, you may want to lope on in to one of these eateries right after you finish those miles.

BLUE HERON: 1123 Lake Street (Emerson and Lake), Minneapolis. Phone 823-4743. Hours: Tues., Wed., Sat., 11 a.m.–9 p.m., Thurs. & Fri.; 11–11 Sun.; 10 a.m.–9 p.m. (brunch served until 3)

This is a self-serve restaurant with a soup and sandwich menu. You place your order at the counter and pick it up when your name is called. No smoking is allowed. Live music is frequently played: on one early autumn lunch-hour, a single flutist played ethereal unaccompanied melodies. Patrons are encouraged to leave tips for the musican(s) in a glass in the middle of each table. A bulletin board on the wall near the entrance features scraps of haiku poetry composed by diners.

The food is very good, but expensive. A small salad of the sort that might accompany a dinner is $2.35. Carrot-raisin bread is excellent but $.60 a slice — and not the size of Wonder Bread either. The best bargain is carob balls for dessert, at $.35 for two. They are delicious, consisting of an uncounted number of health-giving ingredients including miscellaneous grains, coconut, raisins and nuts. One could go far with a couple of carob balls.

The Blue Heron is especially notable for its soups: it serves three different kinds daily: one cream, one bean, and one broth-based. Among the soups have been curried carrot, broccoli bean, onion panade, and rice miso. If you like what you eat, the proprietor will give you the recipe; it'll help you transform those limp or scabrous veggie remnants in your refrigerator into something memorable.

CAFE KARDAMENA: 364 Selby, St. Paul. Phone 224-2209. Open Tues.–Sat., 11 a.m.–9 p.m. Closed Sunday and Monday.

This is a pleasant place by day, with brick walls, and wooden tables and chairs, but it is a bit dreary by night. It needs either more light or light closer to the tables or, better yet, candles.

The menu includes several good salads — garden, fruit and Greek — and two soups du jour: "one from the field and one from the garden." There are lots of juices and teas available, and some of Kardamena's sandwiches are similar enough to children's favorites to be acceptable to fickle youngsters. Tuna, grilled cheese, and egg salad are among the offerings. Desserts include carob sundaes and sweet potato pie. (The latter tastes just like a good, well-spiced pumpkin pie to all but the most sensitive palates.)

FINLAYSON'S: 2221 West 50th Street (50th and Penn), Minneapolis. Phone 927-4416. Open MWTh 4–10:30 p.m.; Fri., 4 p.m.–12; Sat., 12–12; Sun., 4–9 p.m. Closed Tuesdays.

Finlayson's is a modified vegetarian restaurant. It serves fish and seafood, but no red meat. It has a variety of Italian entrees, including such items as linguine and veggie pizza, and boasts that its fresh fish and seafood are flown in daily from one coast or another.

Fin's soups and desserts are homemade, and if you are not careful you can undo a week of prudence and brisk running with a single piece of their excellent banana cream pie.

Beverages include a variety of herb teas, fruit juices, and mineral waters, as well as a mediocre lemonade. Smoking is permitted, but there is a separate room for non-smokers. The service is quick and attentive, the food is fresh and well-prepared, and the menu includes many items not commonly found even in vegetarian restaurants.

Finlayson is only a couple of blocks south of Lake Harriet, and only a few blocks from Minnehaha Parkway, both favorite locations in which to run.

GREAT EXPECTATIONS: 1671 Selby, St. Paul. Phone 644-1836. Open 7 days: M–Th, 10:30–9 p.m.; Fri. & Sat. to 10 p.m. Brunch served Sat. 7–10:30 a.m.; Sun. til 2 p.m.

Great Expectations is not strictly speaking a vegetarian restaurant: one can obtain hamburgers here, for example in addition to the omelettes, salads, and open-face veggie sandwiches that are the mainstays of the menu. This is a convenience for the family that includes calorie-conscious vegetarian runners AND young children who believe that only hamburgers and French fries are really edible. The fries, incidentally, are the skin-on kind, and they are delicious.

Beverages include cider, coffee and tea — no mineral waters. Desserts include carrot cake and cheesecake: the latter is excellent, the former of indifferent quality and not the equal of the Mud Pie's for example.

Two attractive features of Great Expectations are its Sunday brunch, which will not empty your pocketbook, and its willingness to serve half portions of its sandwiches and salads.

The decor of Great Expectations is simple, with a country charm: floors are in their natural state, booths are wooden, and the plants and miscellaneous greenery are not so abundant that you feel they are significantly reducing the oxygen level in the restaurant. Be sure to look at the plant loft — an ingenious touch, new to this diner.

MORNINGSIDE CAFE (formerly Prashad Kitchen): 3415 West 44th, Minneapolis; 926-7890. Open 11 a.m.–9 p.m., M–Th, weekends until 10 p.m. Sunday brunch

Prashad, a vegetarian and natural foods restaurant that's been around since 1974, changed ownership and management late in 1979. The new incarnation is similar to the old. The decor is the same, a pleasant mixture of late Victorian and art deco. The china and silver are still unpretentious: the kind one might get for the lake cottage from secondhand stores. And, as in the old Prashad, only about 1/3 of what is on the menu is actually available. By the spring of 1980, the new proprietor promises, what you see there will be what you can get. That will include tabouli, guacamole, Greek salad, and stuffed pita.

In late winter, the Mexican entrees, veggie sandwiches on good whole wheat bread, and the cream soups were the best bets. Desserts included carrot cake and several varieties of cheesecake.

MUD PIE: 2549 Lyndale Avenue South, Minneapolis, 55404; 823-3432. Open M–Sat, 11 a.m.–1 a.m. Closed Sundays.

Mud Pie has attractive wooden booths, an understated Mexican decor, and an outdoor garden restaurant section that is shielded from the street by a high board fence.

The menu is varied, and all of it is excellent. It includes some Mexican, Arabian and Oriental entrees as well as sandwiches and salads. The carrot cake is superb. Beverages include wine and beer as well as mineral waters, fruit juices, and teas. The food is well prepared, the atmosphere is very pleasant. To more than one diner's mind, this is the best veggie restaurant in Minneapolis.

FAST FOOD RESTAURANTS

Sooner or later, even the most dedicated and abstemious runner may be compelled to dine at a fast food eatery. There are two things you can do: throw caution to the winds and pig out on the old favorites: for example, a 15-piece bucket of the Colonel's chicken, is 3300 calories, a Big Mac and French fries are 775, or an Arby's Super roast beef sandwich is 705. If the very thought repels you, you can make the best of a bad situation by choosing your meal more carefully. Here are some suggestions:

Arby's: The junior roast beef sandwich is only 240 calories.

Burger King: Stay away from the Whopper — 606 calories — and select a hamburger (252) or hot dog (291) instead.

Colonel Sanders' Kentucky Fried Chicken: Don't do it! But if you must, remember one drumstick is 220 calories; a 3-piece special 660.

Dairy Queen: The news is better than you might expect. DQ uses ice milk; therefore, a small cone has only 113, a medium one 225, and a large one 339.

Hardee's: A fish sandwich at 275 calories is your best choice.

McDonald's: A hamburger here is 249. The Filet-o-Fish is not as low in calories here as the fish sandwich is at Hardee's. It rings in at 406. If you're at the Golden Arches for breakfast, you'll find the Egg McMuffin is 312 calories.

Taco Bell: One taco is only 159 calories; a tostado is 188. From here on, the count escalates: a bellburger is 243, a burrito is 319, and an enchilada is 418. If you can persuade your fast-food lovers to join you in a trip to a Taco Bell, you'll probably do better here than anywhere else.

Arthur Treacher's Fish and Chips: an order of fish and chips is 275.

White Castle: One hamburger has 157 calories; a fish sandwich has only 200, and a milk shake only 213. The prices are low too.

RACES

There's no need for you to ever enter a race, but the time may come when you want to measure yourself against other runners or simply to run with a lot of company. Veterans remember the days when a race brought out twenty people, all of whom knew each other. Today, there are races in the Twin Cities that routinely attract thousands. Some are well-organized, some are not. Some corporate sponsors of races are genuinely interested in running; some hardly know the left shoe from the right and care only that you advertise their product on your T-shirt. When you begin racing you may not mind the huckster qualities that sometimes creep in the mega-races. Eventually, however, you will probably hit the wall — the limit of your own capacity to endure commercialization — and you may choose to avoid the more offensive and/or badly organized contests.

The Minnesota Distance Running Association, in cooperation with Sole Sports, running stores, has a 24-hour Raceline number — 822-5007 which you can call to hear what races are being run in the area each week and how and where you can register. Raceline, like the MDRA's quarterly publication, *Minnesota Distance Runner*, includes races outside of the Twin Cities. You might want to plan weekend excursions to include the Smelt Run in Duluth, or the Syttende Mai contest in Grantsburg, Wis.

The contests described here are a few of the more interesting ones. You can find races in Minneapolis or St. Paul every weekend from spring through fall, and through the winter at least once or twice a month. April and October are probably the most desirable times to race in Minnesota, but no month is impossible.

Winter Sports Day 4-Mile: It'll probably be cold and it may be sloppy, but this race might be just the mid-winter motivator you need. The race is held in Langford Park in St. Paul, and it's part of a day-long schedule of activities.

Valentine Mixed-Doubles Relay 5-Mile: This February race begins at Pracna-on-Main restaurant, in the river-front area of Minneapolis near St. Anthony Falls. Awards are made in interesting categories, suitable to the holiday being celebrated.

St. Patrick's Day Mini-Marathon 5-1/2 mile: Held at St. Thomas College, for the wearing of the green.

Mud Ball: This MDRA-members-only contest is held in April in Theodore Wirth Park. A hilly trail course, there is also a swamp section that you must slog through. In 1979 the Mud Ball had an extra hazard: for reasons not adequately explained by NSP, several runners received electric shocks as they plunged into the muddy pit. The distance is 4 miles. The conditions are unforgettable.

Fred Kurtz Memorial 10-Mile Handicap: The oldest continuous race in the MDRA schedule, the Fred Kurtz is named after one of the original members. It is run on the East River Road in St. Paul early in April. New rules oblige you to have previous race experience to enter this one, so that handicapping can be equitable.

Get in Gear 10K: This is the first of the giant races each spring. Several thousand runners turn out for the 10K and several thousand more for the two-mile fun run. Both are held on the West River Road late in April. It is well-advertised in local newspapers and sponsored by several local orgnizations. Age-group awards consist of merchandise — shoes, running bags, etc.

Mom's Day 4-Mile: The Mom's Day begins in Riverside Park and ends just across the Franklin Avenue Bridge at Franklin and West River Road. Held on Mother's Day Sunday in mid-May, this race awards a potted plant to each finisher. The river road course isn't difficult after you get past the long hill at the beginning.

Lowry Hill Climb: A five-mile race held late in May, it's not quite as vertical as its name suggests. It begins on Kenwood Parkway, at Parade Stadium, and the climb starts only ¼ of a mile into the race. Then you descend to Lake of the Isles, and the course levels off until you have to climb once more just before the home stretch. A nice feature of this race is that there is an award to the runner who has most improved his or her time from the previous year's Lowry Hill Climb. This would therefore be a good race to inaugurate your racing career.

Diet Pepsi 10K: Another large race, this one is held in mid-June, and age-group winners receive a trip to the Diet Pepsi finals held at world corporate headquarters. The course is the same as the Get In Gear. It runs from Minnehaha Park northward on West River Road to Lake

Street, over the bridge and back along East River Road. There's an awful lot of Diet Pepsi around at this race, but one does *not* feel drowned in a sea of commercial exploitation. Each finisher receives, by mail, his or her computerized Diet Pepsi Rating: it includes your official time, the median time for all participants, and your place within your age/sex group.

Bonne Bell 10K: Women only. About 1300 took part in the July 1979 race, which is held along the route of the Diet Pepsi and the Get in Gear. In addition to age-group awards, the best mother-daughter team receives a prize, and so does the best sister-sister team. The race is sponsored by the cosmetic company, but Bonne Bell's corporate leadership cares about running and is knowledgeable about it as well.

Raspberry Run 5 Mile: Although held in Hopkins, this is an MDRA-sponsored race and attracts mostly Minneapolis and St. Paul runners, so it is included here. It is a hot weather race, so train accordingly. It begins at 1 p.m. on an afternoon in late July, when Hopkins celebrates its Raspberry Festival. Before suburbanization, the town was the "raspberry capital of the world." Shopping centers and neighborhoods have since choked out the raspberries, but the festival and the race are good fun.

Aquatennial 8 mile and 2 mile: This race, too, is associated with a summer festival, the Minneapolis Aquatennial, and it's held in late July. It begins in the evening, however, so if you hate the heat but want to race, choose this contest instead of the Raspberry Run. It is held at Lake of the Isles, more convenient to energy-conscious city-dwellers than the Hopkins race.

Hennepin-Lake Classic: 5K and 10K: You could set a personal record for either of these distances on this course, because it is perfectly flat except for one short, modest hill. It's an August race, however, and can be hot, so don't get your hopes up too high! The route is around Lake Calhoun.

City of Lakes Marathon: A certified marathon, held in October, this race's course consists of four loops around Lake Calhoun and Lake Harriet. It's nearly all flat, so times can be good. If you're only a spectator you can see excellent local and regional talent competing here.

Y-to-Y Halloween Run: Co-sponsored by the YMCAs of Minneapolis and St. Paul, this run begins in downtown Minneapolis and goes either to the University of Minnesota campus (2 miles), the College of St. Thomas (10K) or the state capitol in St. Paul (20K). If you've always harbored a secret desire to run through a city's downtown streets practically in your underwear, this is the race for you. Age-group awards are made for all three distances.

Twin City Track Club Turkey Trot: A 10K around Lake Calhoun, entrants are eligible for the drawing that awards Thanksgiving turkeys to the lucky winners.

Remember: These are only a few of the available races. Call Raceline (822-5007) to find out what's happening the week or weeks you want to run. Any running store in the Twin Cities also posts notices of upcoming races and lists of finishers in past contests.

RUNNING CLUBS

The Minnesota Distance Running Association sponsors or coordinates a wide variety of events including road races, trail and track events, and cross-country contests for runners of all ages and abilities. Members receive a subscription to the quarterly publication, *Minnesota Distance Runner*, and are entitled to participate in several members-only races during the year. For membership information write: MDRA, P.O. Box 14064, University Station, Minneapolis, Mn. 55414.

The MDRA is not a competitive club. Several clubs in the Twin Cities are:

AAU-AFFILIATED CLUBS

Northern Lights Track Club (women only): Sandy Green, 4143 12th Av. S., Minneapolis, 55406; 724-7615. Publishes a monthly newsletter in addition to sponsoring some races and fun runs.

Real World University Track Club: Charlie Quimby, 3428 Portland Av. S., Minneapolis, Mn 55407; 822-1661.

Twin Cities Track Club: Brian Racette, 3515 Homes Av., Minneapolis, Mn. 55408; 822-2864.

Collegeville Track Club: Timothy J. Miles, 1408 West Arlington Av., St. Paul, Mn. 55108; 644-4181.

Mudrunners Track Club: Brad Kingery, 831 Marquette, Minneapolis; 333-4832.

NON-AAU CLUBS

11 O'Clock Club: Bob Trainor, 1310 France Avenue S., Mpls. 55416; 374-1642.

Minnehaha Marathoners: Doug Laird, Box 24336, Minneapolis; 926-0743

Notes

Notes

BIBLIOGRAPHY

Empson, Donald, *The Street Where You Live* (St. Paul: Witsend Press, 1975)

Flanagan, Barbara, *Minneapolis* (New York: St. Martin's Press, 1973)

Gebhard, David and Martinson, Tom, *A Guide to the Architecture of Minnesota* (Minneapolis: University of Minnesota Press, 1977)

Holmquist, June D., and Brookins, Jean, *Minnesota's Major Historic Sites* (St. Paul: Minnesota Historical Society Press, 1972)

Koblas, John, *F. Scott Fitzgerald: His Homes and Haunts*, (St. Paul: Minnesota Historical Society Press, 1978)

Kunz, Virginia B., *St. Paul: Saga of an American City* (Woodland Hills, Calif.: Windsor Publications, 1977)

Lanegran, David A., and Sandeen, Ernest R., *The Lake District of Minneapolis* (St. Paul: Living Historical Museum, 1979)

Lutter, Judy and Erbes, Kathie, *Scouting Energy* (St. Paul: Girl Scout Council of St. Croix Valley, 1979)

Minnesota Distance Runner, 1978 and 1979 issues

Roth, Peter, *Running USA* (New York: Aardvark Books, 1979)

Sandeen, Ernest, *St. Paul's Historic Summit Avenue* (St. Paul: Living Historical Museum, 1978)

Stuhler, Barbara and Kreuter, Gretchen, *Women of Minnesota: Selected Biographical Essays* (St. Paul: Minnesota Historical Society Press, 1977)

Weiner, Lynn, "Our Sister's Keepers: The Minneapolis Woman's Christian Association and Housing for Working Women," *Minnesota History*, Spring 1979, pp. 189–200